Napa Valley & Sonoma

HEART OF THE CALIFORNIA WINE COUNTRY

by VIRGINIE BOONE

NORTHLAND PUBLISHING

CONTENTS

Napa Valley Trip
June '04

Introduction

FOR MANY, NORTHERN CALIFORNIA'S WINE country has a romantic appeal. Its allure brings travelers from all over the world, where they stroll casually among the vines, try tantalizing wines, or savor a gourmet meal. New experiences are as endless as the vineyards.

While in Wine Country, celebrate the annual Mustard Festival in Napa; take a tram up to Sterling Vineyards to taste the new releases and admire the views; collect a picnic basket full of cheese, bread, fruit, and warm brownies from the Oakville Grocery; or hike to the top of the Mayacamas mountain range, which gracefully peers into Napa Valley on one side and into Sonoma Valley on the other. The Wine Country is a feeling, a respite from the rigors of daily life, and an insight into the agricultural way of life that has existed here for centuries. It is about the people who make their lives here—the winemakers, the dairy farmers, the chefs—who love this quieter way of life intricately tied to the land. A sense of place richly colors the Wine Country, whether passing through for the first time or the fiftieth.

The beauty is breathtaking. Imagine a fall drive through an out-of-the-way vineyard, when the leaves have changed colors and harvest is fully under way. A picnic, a sunset, a deep red bottle of Cabernet Sauvignon, the aroma blending with the delicate cheeses and warm bread. It's all here— the wine, the food, the beauty, the romance.

The vineyards of Carneros lie closest to San Francisco's San Pablo Bay and its legendary fog, which helps to produce a cooler climate perfect for Pinot Noir.

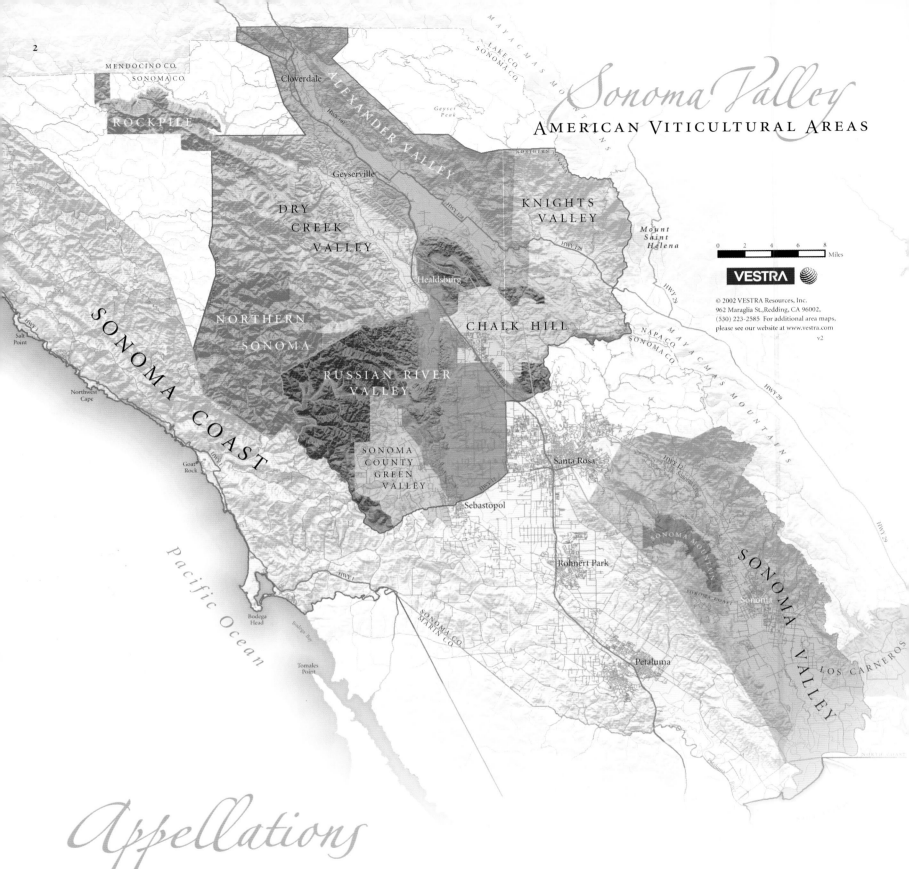

MENDOCINO CO.
SONOMA CO.

ROCKPILE

Cloverdale

ALEXANDER VALLEY

Sonoma Valley

AMERICAN VITICULTURAL AREAS

Geyserville

DRY
CREEK
VALLEY

KNIGHTS
VALLEY

*Mount
Saint
Helena*

Healdsburg

NORTHERN

SONOMA

CHALK HILL

SONOMA COAST

RUSSIAN RIVER
VALLEY

SONOMA
COUNTY
GREEN
VALLEY

Santa Rosa

SONOMA MOUNTAIN

Sebastopol

Rohnert Park

SONOMA VALLEY

Pacific Ocean

Bodega
Head

Sonoma

Petaluma

LOS CARNEROS

0   2   4   6   8
Miles

VESTRA

© 2002 VESTRA Resources, Inc.
962 Maraglia St., Redding, CA 96002,
(530) 223-2585 For additional area maps,
please see our website at www.vestra.com
v2

Appellations

The identifying name found on a wine bottle is there to signify where a wine's grapes have been grown. It designates a specific geographical place as big as a state or as little as one hillside, each with its own weather, soil, and elevation that give the wine a particular flavor. In the U.S., the breakdown of growing regions, or appellations, is controlled by the Bureau of Alcohol, Tobacco, and Firearms (BATF), which has officially delineated the boundaries of the appellations since 1979. To date, 145 American Viticultural Areas (AVAs), or wine growing regions, have been designated across twenty-six states; California has close to ninety.

For a wine to be labeled with the "Napa Valley" appellation, at least eighty-five percent of the grapes in the wine have to come from Napa Valley. If the AVA is larger, like "Sonoma County," at least seventy-five percent of the grapes have to be grown in that area. The BATF does not regulate what kind of grape can be grown within an appellation (unlike government regulators in France), so Cabernet Sauvignon can be grown in Napa, Sonoma, Mendocino, or anywhere else, nor does it limit how much can be grown. However, if a wine is labeled "Cabernet Sauvignon," it has to be composed of at least seventy-five percent of that variety.

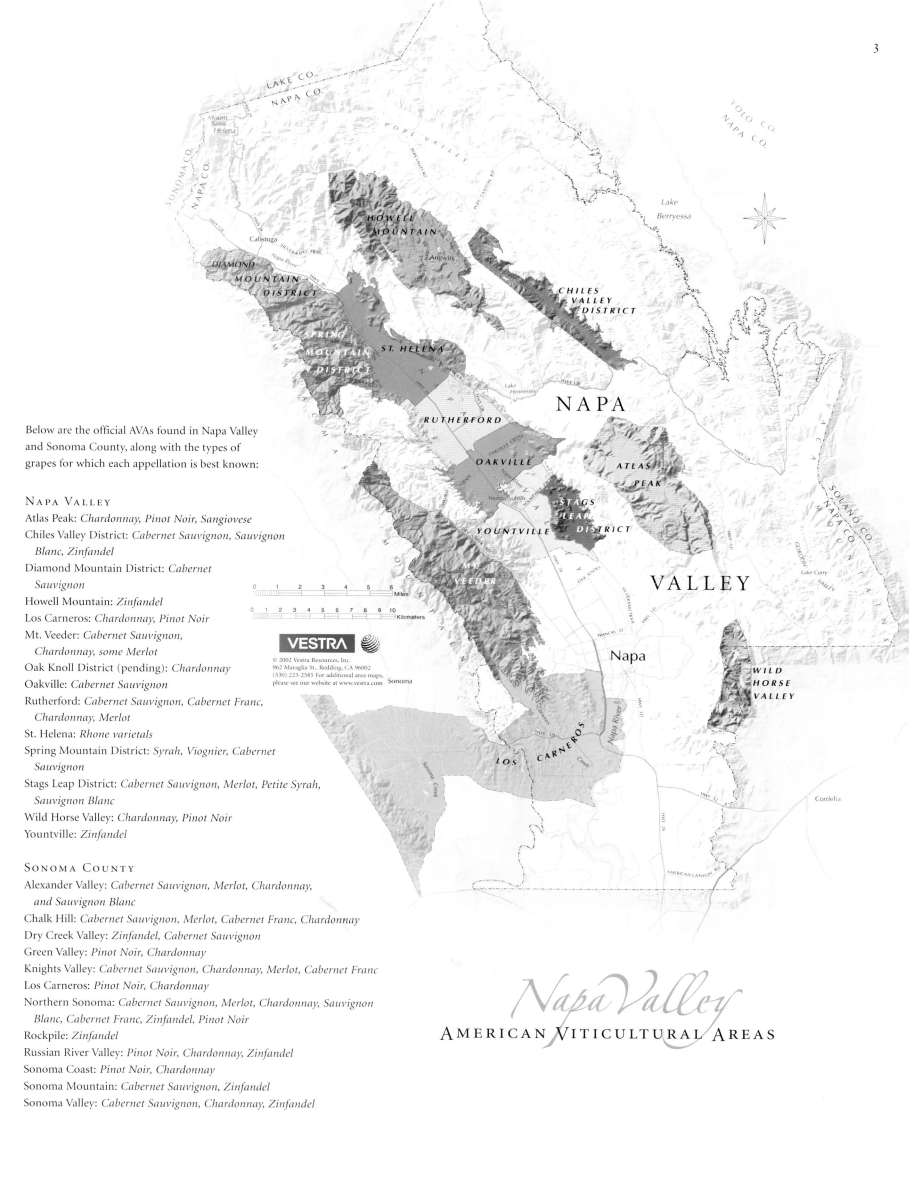

Below are the official AVAs found in Napa Valley and Sonoma County, along with the types of grapes for which each appellation is best known:

Napa Valley

Atlas Peak: *Chardonnay, Pinot Noir, Sangiovese*
Chiles Valley District: *Cabernet Sauvignon, Sauvignon Blanc, Zinfandel*
Diamond Mountain District: *Cabernet Sauvignon*
Howell Mountain: *Zinfandel*
Los Carneros: *Chardonnay, Pinot Noir*
Mt. Veeder: *Cabernet Sauvignon, Chardonnay, some Merlot*
Oak Knoll District (pending): *Chardonnay*
Oakville: *Cabernet Sauvignon*
Rutherford: *Cabernet Sauvignon, Cabernet Franc, Chardonnay, Merlot*
St. Helena: *Rhone varietals*
Spring Mountain District: *Syrah, Viognier, Cabernet Sauvignon*
Stags Leap District: *Cabernet Sauvignon, Merlot, Petite Syrah, Sauvignon Blanc*
Wild Horse Valley: *Chardonnay, Pinot Noir*
Yountville: *Zinfandel*

Sonoma County

Alexander Valley: *Cabernet Sauvignon, Merlot, Chardonnay, and Sauvignon Blanc*
Chalk Hill: *Cabernet Sauvignon, Merlot, Cabernet Franc, Chardonnay*
Dry Creek Valley: *Zinfandel, Cabernet Sauvignon*
Green Valley: *Pinot Noir, Chardonnay*
Knights Valley: *Cabernet Sauvignon, Chardonnay, Merlot, Cabernet Franc*
Los Carneros: *Pinot Noir, Chardonnay*
Northern Sonoma: *Cabernet Sauvignon, Merlot, Chardonnay, Sauvignon Blanc, Cabernet Franc, Zinfandel, Pinot Noir*
Rockpile: *Zinfandel*
Russian River Valley: *Pinot Noir, Chardonnay, Zinfandel*
Sonoma Coast: *Pinot Noir, Chardonnay*
Sonoma Mountain: *Cabernet Sauvignon, Zinfandel*
Sonoma Valley: *Cabernet Sauvignon, Chardonnay, Zinfandel*

Napa Valley
AMERICAN VITICULTURAL AREAS

I

The Wine Country

TO A LOT OF PEOPLE, California Wine Country and Napa are two words that mean the same thing. The truth is that Wine Country in Northern California is Napa and so much more. It is an intricate patchwork of appellations that span across three counties. Most visitors start with the Napa Valley, a compact vision of rolling vineyards and stately wineries about an hour north of San Francisco. Sonoma County, which is closer to the coast than Napa, is bigger and more diverse. Winemaking there is centered around the Sonoma Valley, the Russian River area, and Healdsburg. The northernmost region is Mendocino County, where the Anderson Valley wine region has made inroads of its own.

The Napa Valley is at its widest thirteen miles across and nearly forty miles long, about 754 square miles in all. It stretches from the point at which the Napa River empties into San Pablo Bay north to the mountains above Calistoga, where heated mineral waters from geothermal activity have long lured vacationers. The Napa River cuts through the length of the Valley and is navigable all the way to the city of Napa. The Valley itself has volcanic origins and gold, silver, and cinnabar have all been mined at one time or another.

Left: **Carneros' rolling vineyards soak up the midday sun, vital to the growth of all these grapes.** *Right:* **A sign in Sonoma points the way to some of the region's best wineries.**

The Mayacamas mountain range is to the west; its peaks include Mount Veeder and Spring Mountain. The east is bound by the Vaca Range and volcanic Howell Mountain. The Valley's highest peak is 4,344-foot Mount St. Helena at the northern end of the valley.

The Valley enjoys warm summers and mild winters, and even when the summer heat gets up into the 100s, the area is tempered by early morning and late evening fog. Napa's main towns are: Napa, Yountville, Oakville, Rutherford, St. Helena, and Calistoga. Thanks in part to the success of the wine industry and the acres of vineyards it requires, Napa's population is a low 128,145 with a density of 164 people per square mile. The Napa Valley is its own wine appellation, and though forty-four different red and twenty-eight white wine grape varieties are successfully grown here, Napa is particularly suited to the growing of Cabernet Sauvignon grapes. Just say the words "Napa Valley Cab" and see a wine lover's eyes light up.

Sonoma shares a border with Napa and runs in roughly the same direction but is more than double its size at fifty-eight miles long and twenty-four miles wide, or 1,576 square miles altogether.

Top: **Main Street in St. Helena dates back to 1853, when free lots were offered to anyone willing to open a business.** *Below:* **Sonoma's City Hall today.** *Bottom:* **City Hall being built in 1909.** *Opposite:* **Napa Valley's highest peak, Mt. St. Helena, as seen from the top of Sterling Winery.** *Pages 8-9:* **Beautiful old Oaks are a common sight among the vineyards of Sonoma's Valley of the Moon.**

A county with a broad range of physical traits, climates, and agricultural uses, it has almost the same amount of land planted with vines. The Mayacamas, in this case, are to the east, and the Sonoma Mountains are to the west, protecting the Valley from fog off the Pacific Ocean. Carneros, a wine region at the southern end of the Valley, is shared by Napa and Sonoma. It touches the San Pablo Bay, and as a result, it has the coolest temperatures, a factor that prolongs the growing season, making it an ideal area for Pinot Noir and Chardonnay grapes.

Sonoma County has several centers of activity. The main towns in Sonoma Valley include Sonoma, Glen Ellen, and Kenwood, and west of the Valley are the population centers of Petaluma and Santa Rosa. North from Santa Rosa are Wine Country towns such as Healdsburg and Geyserville and the wine growing region of Alexander Valley. From Santa Rosa to the Sonoma Coast are the Russian River Valley towns of Sebastopol, Forestville, and Guerneville, all of which are cool in the winter and get their fair share of fog. And finally, along the coast are lightly populated beach hamlets like Bodega Bay and Jenner. Sonoma County's population is close to 465,000 or 291 people per square mile.

Mendocino County is to the north of Sonoma, just past the inland town of Cloverdale or Sea Ranch on the coast. It is a huge, sparsely populated county, marked by rolling hills, stands of redwood trees, and a very rugged coastline. The county population of 87,000, or twenty-five people per square mile, is focused in the southernmost section where grapes are grown, about 13,000 acres in all. Chardonnay is the number one varietal grown here, followed by Zinfandel and Cabernet Sauvignon.

Anderson Valley lies within Mendocino County starting at the town of Boonville, which is close to three hours north of San Francisco. The rolling pastures used to be used for cattle and sheep ranching, but have now mostly given way to vineyards. Anderson Valley vineyards lie at an elevation of about 375 feet and are marked by a foggy, coastal climate, actually the coolest climate in which grapes can be successfully grown. Days are warm and sunny, while nights see their fair share of cool fog. Pinot Noir and Chardonnay thrive here, as well as a limited amount of Syrah, Riesling, and Gewürztraminer.

All told, these different sections of Northern California make up some of the most beautiful country in the West, and the landscapes, the cuisine, and especially the wine, draw visitors from all over the world. As many found out long ago, one visit to California's breathtaking Wine Country will never be enough.

Top: Sonoma County's diverse landscape includes groves of Redwoods. *Bottom:* The Petaluma landscape remains relatively vineyard-free, inhabited more frequently by dairy cows and roaming horses.
Opposite Top: Jagged Rock Islands off the Mendocino Coast dot the ocean view.
Opposite Bottom: The Mendocino Coast waits gracefully for sunset.

2

History in the Making

CALIFORNIA'S WINE COUNTRY was originally inhabited by several different indigenous groups. The word "Napa" is often ascribed to the Suisan tribe and is said to mean "motherland," which is an appropriate name given that food was so plentiful.

The luscious soil, Mediterranean climate, and availability of water brought more settlers, starting with the Spanish, who first set foot in the area in the early 1600s. But the new inhabitants didn't truly start to settle "Alta California" until around 1769, when they built presidios and a series of missions to be run by Franciscan monks. By the end of the Spanish colonial period in California, there would be presidios in Monterey, San Francisco, and Santa Barbara, as well as over twenty missions scattered throughout the state. Many of the missions planted grapes to make wine for ceremonial purposes, using a grape variety that came to be called the "Mission" grape, which made a mediocre red. When Mexico gained its independence from Spain in 1821, it also gained control of Alta California and began to more actively develop the land. In 1823, the Mexicans built the San Francisco de Solano Mission in what is now the town of Sonoma.

Left: **The chapel at Christian Brothers Retreat Center at Mont La Salle in Napa patiently watches over its rolling vineyards.** *Right:* **The historic Sonoma Mission.**

Opposite: **Dr. Edward Turner Bale's 1840s grist mill near Calistoga is now a state park.**
Above: **A monument to Sonoma's Bear Flag Rebellion stands in the town's central plaza.**

They established it as their governmental center for the north with General Mariano Vallejo acting as the government's representative in charge.

Mexico encouraged settlement in this region by granting big plots of land known as ranchos, most of which were used first to graze cattle. One of the earliest plots to be issued by General Vallejo was to George C. Yount, a North Carolinian who came to California in 1831 looking to hunt and trap. Yount had to become a Mexican citizen, as well as be baptized into the Catholic Church in order to qualify for the land grant, but by 1836 he qualified and was given an 11,000-acre plot known as Rancho Caymus, an area that spanned the northern edge of modern-day Yountville all the way to the center of Napa Valley.

Around the same time, Dr. Edward Turner Bale set foot in the Valley. In 1841, he was granted a large sum of land north of Yount's ranch, which included present-day St. Helena and Calistoga. He built the Bale Grist Mill on the property to ground grain into flour.

But most land still belonged to Mexico, and new settlers without it started to demand a change. Their restlessness coincided with America's sudden imperative of Manifest Destiny and the success of Texas in gaining independence from Mexico in 1836. Their desire for a piece of California culminated in the Bear Flag Rebellion, a quick attempt by American settlers to take California from Mexico. In 1846, a group of thirty-three men traveled from Sutter's Fort to Sonoma, captured General Vallejo (who would later help form the new state government), took the Mexican flag down, put a new Bear Republic flag up, and celebrated.

Westward migration flooded the Southwest throughout the 1840s, but the 1848 discovery of gold at Sutter's Mill in the Sierra Mountains changed everything. The resulting Treaty of Guadalupe Hidalgo made California an official U.S. territory, and by the end of 1849, over 80,000 gold diggers had made their way to the state. Napa County soon responded to the overwhelming demand for wheat, and by the time California was incorporated as a state in 1850, it was big enough to be one of the original twenty-seven counties. By 1852, the town of Napa alone had 300 citizens.

In 1853, the town of St. Helena was formed when an Englishman named Henry Still bought one hundred acres of land, opened a small store, and offered free lots to anyone who would build a business on their property. Roads were constructed to help haul grain and flour to ferries, which also shipped out cattle hides and quicksilver from the local mines. By 1859, steamboats regularly traveled between Napa and San Francisco in three hours.

Though wheat was king, some residents tried to diversify. JM Pachett came to Napa in the mid 1850s, where he bought land and planted vines. He hired a young Prussian named Charles Krug to help him press the grapes into wine using a cider press. Together they produced 1,200 gallons of wine, the first production of Napa Valley wine since Spanish times, when grapes had been pressed by foot.

A few years later, Krug bought land of his own and added the expertise of a forward-thinking Hungarian immigrant named Count Agoston Haraszthy. Haraszthy had just established the first commercial winery in California, the Buena Vista Winery, which is still in business today. Most importantly, Haraszthy was the first grower in the area to plant Vitis vinifera, or grapes specifically intended for wine, instead of varietal grapes grown for eating.

Krug soon married the daughter of Dr. Bale and was given 540 acres of land north of St. Helena as part of her dowry, and with it he set out to seriously make wine. In the process, he became one of the most vocal advocates for winemaking in Napa Valley, and by the mid 1860s, over 1,000 acres in Napa were planted in grapes. There was so much activity that Krug created the St. Helena-based Viticultural Club to exchange expertise and lobby for the nascent wine industry. Among the club's members were growers George Belden Crane, who urged others to plant *Vinis vinifera* instead of other varietal grapes, especially the more common Mission grape; Jacob Schram, who started Schramsberg in 1862; and Jacob Beringer, who was Krug's former cellar foreman. In 1877, Beringer bought acreage of his own and established Beringer Brothers Winery with his brother Fredrick.

Above: **Many credit Agoston Haraszthy, a Hungarian immigrant, as the founder of California's wine industry.** *Left:* **The Charles Krug Winery north of St. Helena was one of the first in the Napa Valley.** *Below:* **St. Helena's original Main Street, complete with a bank, hotel, and saloon, circa 1880.**

Top: A barge stands docked along the Napa River, ready to be loaded with grapes. River transport was key to developing California's wine industry. *Above:* A historic label from Inglenook, once the king of Napa wines. *Bottom:* Count Haraszthy's world-renown caves at the Buena Vista Winery in Sonoma. *Pages 18-19:* The robust Napa River provides needed nourishment to the famous vineyards of the Napa Valley, traveling 50 miles from Mt. St. Helena to the San Pablo Bay.

As vines were planted and wine was made, Gold Rush supplier Sam Brannan found his way to Calistoga in the 1860s and built a resort around the area's natural hot springs and mineral waters. His idea took off and soon the Napa Valley Railroad was being constructed to connect Calistoga to Napa, where steamboats now brought steady visitors from San Francisco. The railroad also transported grain, grapes, and, in time, wine.

Sonoma's efforts to develop were hampered by a lack of transportation, something that Napa was quick to exploit. The Napa River was a crucial link to the San Pablo Bay and the metropolitan hub of San Francisco, a burgeoning market for the Valley's products. And finally, the introduction of the transcontinental railroad in 1869 made it possible to reach prosperous East Coast markets as well.

The new transportation infrastructure and a steady stream of visitors kept the wine industry going, and the two decades after 1870 were a time of marked growth in the California wine industry. Among the renowned wineries built during this time were Beringer, Far Niente, Greystone, Inglenook, and Chateau Montelena.

The 1870s were a period of significant growth in the Sonoma wine industry, as well, with thousands of acres being planted from San Pablo Bay northward to Glen Ellen. Count Haraszthy's Buena Vista Winery grew to over 500 acres, making it one of the largest vineyards in California. Other Sonoma-based wineries that came into prominence around this time were Gundlach-Bundschu and, just after the turn of the century, Sebastiani Vineyards, established in 1904 on a vineyard once owned by General Vallejo.

Wine was already on its way to becoming one of the area's primary commercial products when a phylloxera (pronounced fill-ox-era) epidemic devastated the vines of France, opening an even bigger market for California grapes. By the mid-1880s, production from 140 wineries reached 5 million gallons and the total number of acres planted in grapes grew to 20,000. By the early-1890s, wine had firmly established itself and Napa wines started to earn honors at international

competitions. Some of the fine wines recognized at this time include Gustave Niebaum's Inglenook and Jacob Schram's Schramsberg.

But fortune did not come to all vintners. Over-production, a depressed economy, and a tax on brandy obliterated some of the efforts of the early wine pioneers, including Krug, who went broke. From 1890 to 1892, production dropped from 5 million gallons to 2 million and overproduction cut grape prices from $24/ton to $8/ton. Then, in 1893, insult was added to injury when Napa was hit by its own bout of phylloxera and half the vineyards were lost, reducing the overall total to about 3,000 acres. Some landowners abandoned vines and opted to grow prunes instead, while others planted olive trees and developed presses to make oil. Other orchards were planted to grow apples and peaches.

By the turn of the century, Napa was still supplying ten percent of the nation's grain needs, and the valley's population reached over 16,000. The wine industry revived once a phylloxera-resistant grapevine was introduced. Wisely, new vintners took advantage of the opportunity to grow new varietals and made innovations in their winemaking processes to produce even better vintages. It was all coming along nicely until 1920, when Prohibition became the Eighteenth Amendment to the U.S. Constitution and the manufacture, distribution, and sale of alcohol was no longer allowed.

Opposite Top: **A lush view of California wine pioneer Robert Mondavi's Spanish Mission-style winery in Oakville.**

Opposite Bottom: **A bottle of Schramsberg sparkling wine. One of Napa's oldest brands, Schramsberg has been making award-winning vintages since 1965.**

Above: **The Beringer Brothers' 17-room Rhine House, an exact replica of their Queen Anne Victorian home in Germany, now serves as the winery's visitors' center.**

Bottom: **Beaulieu Vineyard Winery has been known through the years for its many innovations in winemaking, thanks in part to the essential work of viticulturalist Andre Tchelistcheff.**

Practically overnight, wineries closed and grape acreage fell. But because individuals could still make up to 200 gallons per year for personal use, demand for grapes persisted and, after the initial impact, acreage surprisingly went up. Interestingly, because many home winemakers were across the country, growers were pushed to try different types of grapes that could hold up better in shipping. Thirteen years later, when Prohibition was repealed, Petite Sirah and Zinfandel were the dominant varietals.

Among the wineries that survived Prohibition were Christian Brothers, which was able to sell wine for medicinal and sacramental uses; Beaulieu, where Georges de Latour continued to make Cabernet Sauvignon, aging it in his cellars until the laws changed; Inglenook, which sold its grapes; Beringer, another sacramental wine producer; and Larkmead Vineyards, which also sold grapes and made sacramental wine. Not long after Prohibition's repeal in 1933, Beaulieu's 1940 Private Reserve Cabernet Sauvignon put Napa Cabernet Sauvignon on the world map. Other award-winning wineries soon established were Louis M. Martini and Mondavi, which came into fruition with Cesare Mondavi's purchase of the Charles Krug Winery in 1943. Together, these wineries would help bring Napa wines into worldwide prominence by the 1960s.

Sonoma also enjoyed a post-Prohibition boom, as unions formed and tariff laws were revised. Winemakers there aspired to compete with French wines, and as early as 1934, *The New York Times* singled out wines from Sonoma Valley as worthy.

Progress came in the form of better technology, as well. In 1937, Beaulieu Vineyard Winery hired a scientist by the name of Andre Tchelistcheff after a shipment of wine spoiled en route to the East Coast. The Moscow-born Tchelistcheff had fled the Russian Revolution and was working in the Institute of National Agronomy in Paris, where he had become an expert in enological science and viticulture. At Beaulieu, Tchelistcheff introduced temperature-controlled fermentation, making it possible to successfully store and ship white wine. The importance of making white wine a viable commercial product was key because whites could be delivered to market earlier than reds, allowing a quicker return of cash to a winery, which in turn could be used to fund the growth of more grapes.

Tchelistcheff stayed at Beaulieu until his retirement in 1973. Along the way he became a huge part of the winemaking community and added to the school of winemaking knowledge by staying in touch with viticultural scholars at U.C. Davis. After retiring, he became a consultant for several wineries, helping them to innovate through technology.

The Numbers

Based on year 2000 figures, the numbers behind today's wine industry are staggering. California's wine industry is responsible for $33 billion in revenue, and when you count all the direct and indirect benefits, that makes wine the state's most valued finished product. As a matter of fact, the state makes ninety percent of all wine made in the United States.

The Napa Valley Vintners Association counts 220 wineries as members, while there are said to be an additional 180 wineries in Sonoma County, and these numbers are constantly growing. Vineyards criss-cross 45,000 acres of Napa County, and in Sonoma, the total grape acreage has increased fifty-four percent over the last ten years to total 42,000 acres. Sonoma now has a wide lead over Napa in terms of the actual amount of fruit that is harvested (190,000 tons versus 136,000), but Napa Valley wines are still better known and higher in price. Napa grapes sell for about $2,827 per ton; Sonoma's are worth $2,158. And in both Napa and Sonoma, Chardonnay is the number one white wine grape grown, while Cabernet Sauvignon remains the main red wine grape varietal.

Right: Corks grow from a species of oak tree found predominantly in Spain and Portugal, which produces almost half of the world's commercial cork. The world's annual expenditure on cork is estimated at $100 million.

Above Left: Ivy-covered Chateau Montelena, established in 1882, stands stoically over its estate. *Above Right:* The winery's 1973 Chardonnay scored highest at the famous Paris Tasting of 1976—an event that decisively launched Napa Valley wines to the world.

To this day, he is greatly credited with helping the California wine industry thrive after Prohibition.

The attention garnered by the growing wine industry also attracted outside investors who wanted a piece of the mystique. The 1960s and `70s brought a flurry of investment to the area, cementing it as one of the most important wine regions in the world. With over fifty wineries in operation in the Napa Valley alone, tasting rooms were introduced in 1963. They were such a success that over 500,000 visitors flocked to them that first year. In 1964, the venerated Inglenook Winery was sold to United Vintners, a sure sign that Napa wine had become a respected and marketable commodity. In 1966, Robert and Peter Mondavi split up, leaving Peter to run the Charles Krug Winery, and Robert to start his own winery. In charge of his own destiny, Robert Mondavi worked tirelessly to further promote California wines.

With all that preceded it, Napa's landmark moment would still come down to one year and one event—the Paris Tasting. At this event, an all-French panel of judges set about to compare French and American wines in a blind taste test. Of course, they envisioned the publicity stunt as an excellent way to re-affirm the superiority of Bordeaux and Burgundy wines over upstart, surely inferior California efforts. The panel poured four white Burgundies and four red Bordeaux against six California Chardonnays and six California Cabernet Sauvignons. Scores were noted and the results read, but to everyone's surprise, the winners were not among the French Premier Crus, a category containing the rarest, highest quality Bordeaux

and Burgundy wines, but a 1973 Chardonnay from Chateau Montelena and a 1973 Stag's Leap Wine Cellars Cabernet Sauvignon. These results would instantly define Napa Valley wines as among the best in the world, and critical acclaim and high prices would accompany the wines forever after.

So the stage was set and the industry ready for what would occur in 1991—the year *60 Minutes* chose to air a story innocuously titled "The French Paradox." The story, which described the health benefits of wine (especially red), opened the eyes of a country that had so vehemently enforced Prohibition, and suddenly made it acceptable, even advisable, for Americans to drink wine regularly. Not beer, not whisky, but wine. Wine sales went up and visits to the wine country ballooned. The amount of grapes grown in Napa grew by twenty percent throughout the 1990s, eighty percent of which were composed of Bordeaux red grape varietals such as Cabernet Sauvignon, Cabernet Franc, and Merlot, affirming Napa's ability to call itself "America's Bordeaux" in reputation and reality. By the end of the twentieth century, there were more than 35,000 acres of vines and over 200 wineries in Napa County alone.

Today, the acreage planted in grapevines is already up to 45,000 as wine-minded people continue to come to Napa and Sonoma in search of the ideal winemaking lifestyle. And much like the days of Haraszthy, Krug, Tchelistcheff, and even Robert Mondavi, entrepreneurialism will continue to thrive as vigorously as the grapes, as this whole new generation of brash new winemakers remains determined to define wine in their own creative way.

3

Wine-Making

WINEMAKING IS PART SCIENCE, PART ART, part luck, and part determination. In California, it has always been marked by an independence of spirit and a willingness to learn from what has come before. The result is reflected in each bottle of wine that comes out of the brilliant Napa and Sonoma Valley countryside.

Different varieties of grape clones are used throughout the Wine Country, almost all of which are based on varietals that originated in Europe (Chardonnay and Cabernet Sauvignon being the most commonly grown in both Napa and Sonoma). Zinfandel is the only grape type thought to be purely American, though no one is yet one hundred percent certain of its origins. Starting at the beginning of the twentieth century, European vintners began grafting their vines to American rootstocks, which are not susceptible to Phylloxera, a type of aphid that quickly destroys vines from the ground up. Today, most vines are still grafted in this way, making the majority of plants Phylloxera-resistant.

Left and Below: **Wine glasses are designed in different shapes for different types of wine, based on the theory that the shape will affect how the wine reaches a drinker's taste buds.**

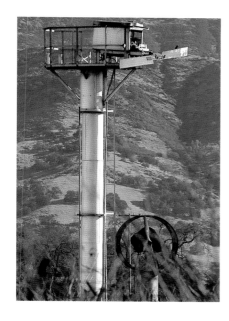

Opposite: **From the air, every inch of the Napa Valley seems to be planted in vineyards; the illusion is not far from the truth.**
Top: **A rolling view of the vineyards at La Famiglia Winery, one of the labels within Robert Mondavi's portfolio. La Famiglia focuses on Italian varietals such as Sangiovese and Barbera.** *Above:* **A vineyard fan protects new buds from the frost.**
Bottom: **The vineyards of Far Niente in Oakville produce fine Chardonnay and Cabernet Sauvignon.**

Vines are happiest at latitudes of thirty to fifty degrees north and thirty to fifty degrees south, and it should be no surprise that climate is absolutely the key ingredient, which is why Napa and Sonoma are so perfectly suited to grapes. The area's proclivity for producing great wine grapes is further enhanced by its disproportionate number of microclimates, which allow a lot of different types of wine to come out of a relatively small area. The average yearly temperature cannot fall below fifty degrees Fahrenheit and frost is especially dangerous in late spring, when it will damage new buds and reduce the size of the crop. In all, close to one hundred days of sunshine are needed from first flowering to first harvest (a ripening period from June to September, usually), in order for the grapes to develop the right amount of sugars. Too little sun will produce grapes high in acid and low in sugar; too much heat results in grapes high in sugar and low in acid. Too much rain toward the end of the ripening period is also a concern, as rain will swell grapes and weaken the juice inside.

Heavy mists and rain can cause grapes to rot, and so a vineyard's soil must be well drained. At the same time, if winters aren't cold enough, diseases and pests survive and can threaten the vines. Lastly, a pattern of hot days and cool nights has to happen—a forty-degree swing is ideal— and the longer the days, the better the grapes.

A wine's appellation is a description of where its grapes have been grown, a specification of the geographic traits, climate, and soils that when mixed together with a winemaker's abilities will produce wine with a particular set of characteristics. Typically, where vines have to struggle for existence, on a rocky hillside, for example, superior wine grapes are produced. Vines have to push their roots further down in search of water and are therefore better able to feed off the trace minerals and elements found below. Deeper roots are also better able to survive severe winter conditions and drought. Vines grown in such conditions will often produce lower yields per vine than those grown on valley floors where water is plentiful, but their grapes will have more flavor and color.

A grape has four basic parts. 1) The pulp produces grape juice, which provides water content, and the sugars and acids in the juice provide the fruit flavor. Sugars are also important to fermentation. 2) Grape skins give red wine its color while the skins, seeds, and stems contain tannins, the crystalline compounds that allow wine to age gracefully. Skins also contain yeasts and bacteria needed in fermentation. 3) Pips, or seeds, hold bitter oils and are discarded after grapes are crushed, yet contribute to tannins beforehand. 4) The grape's stems are usually removed before grapes are crushed or pressed but are sometimes left on for a limited amount of time during fermentation to increase the tannin content in red wines, ultimately improving the wine's overall structure.

Grape Varietals

According to Karen MacNeil's *Wine Bible*, there are thought to be about 5,000 different varieties of grapes (others say 10,000), but of that number only about 150 grape varieties are grown in any substantial amount and known to wine drinkers. The classics can be broken down as such: Cabernet Sauvignon, Merlot, Pinot Noir, Zinfandel, and Syrah for reds and Chardonnay, Chenin Blanc, Riesling, Sauvignon Blanc, and Sémillon for white wines. All of these grape varietals belong to the vinifera species—wine grapes that have been grown in Europe for centuries, but first planted in California in the 1870s by Agoston Haraszthy. The term "varietal" simply means wine made from a specific variety of grape. So wine made from Chardonnay grapes, for example, is a Chardonnay varietal.

There are numerous varietals grown in California, and not all of them are well known. To Americans, lesser known grapes include Viognier, a French white grape making its way through California; Nebbiolo, a popular red grape planted throughout Italy but rarely anywhere else; Sangiovese, the grape behind Chianti wine; Malbec, a red Argentinean grape; and even Cabernet Franc, a grape incredibly important to Bordeaux's reds. All of these, as well as many others, are planted throughout the region, just not nearly to the same degree as the following favorite varietals:

CHARDONNAY

The number one varietal grown in the U.S., this white wine grape is also popular in Australia and South Africa, and is also found in wines from Burgundy, France. Chardonnay is also used in Champagne and other sparkling wines. Chardonnay grapes produce wines that are dry, fruity, rich, and complex, and are often described as "buttery." Often aged in oak barrels, Chardonnay came into its own after Chateau Montelena's 1973 vintage won the Paris Tasting.

CABERNET SAUVIGNON

A robust grape variety known for being fruity, spicy, or herbaceous, and high in tannins, it is considered the king of reds. It is also the same grape grown in France's Bordeaux region, and in 1992, it became the leading red wine grape variety in California. Originally thought to be a cross between Cabernet Franc and Sauvignon Blanc grapes, it is believed that Cabernet Sauvignon grapes first came to California as long ago as 1852, but very little survived Prohibition. Georges de Latour at Beaulieu had the largest holding at that time. The Paris Tasting of 1976 saw a 1973 Stag's Leap Cabernet ignite California's Cabernet Sauvignon reputation and top-end Napa Valley Cabs have commanded top dollar ever since.

MERLOT

Merlot is its own red grape and its own well-known varietal, but Merlot grapes are largely used in blended wines, most specifically in Bordeaux-style blends, such as Cabernet Sauvignon, which often contains up to fifteen percent Merlot. Merlot has a fruity, raspberry-like flavor and full body. Merlot acreage grew at a faster pace in California than any other variety during the late 1980s and 1990s, and it is now the state's third most productive red-wine grape. Growers and winemakers like it because it ripens earlier than Cabernet Sauvignon and thus is less likely to be negatively affected by fall rains. It also makes softer, less tannic wines and requires less cellaring.

PINOT NOIR

This is the red grape found in the great Burgundy wines of France, with a complex, rich flavor and fruity, spicy, and flowery bouquet. Pinot Noir didn't catch on in California until after Prohibition and really didn't come into its own until the mid 1990s. It is not an easy grape to grow and some consider it the most fickle of all varietals—both in the vineyard and the winery. It buds and ripens earlier than other grapes and is susceptible to disease. It likes soils with high concentrations of limestone but hates hot, dry weather which is why it does so well in Carneros and the Russian River Valley, where cool fog is a common sight. French oak barrels are typically used to age Pinot.

ZINFANDEL

This is interestingly the only true American grape. Red Zinfandel is strong and high in tannins and often described as being spicy or tasting like berries. A lot of people find it overpowering, though new cellar techniques are helping to bring Zinfandel to the forefront. White Zinfandels are sourced from the same grapes as Red Zinfandels and are fresh, fruity, and pink. The main difference between the red and white Zinfandels is that the whites do not sit in the skins as long and are not aged in oak. White Zin became popular in the 1970s, and Sutter Home was selling a million cases a year by the mid-1980s.

SAUVIGNON BLANC

This white varietal is best drunk young and is most often described as being "herbaceous." It can also be quite acidic and even smoky. Refreshing and crisp, it is best enjoyed on hot afternoons, with salads or shellfish. Sauvignon Blanc is found in white Bordeaux wines and in the great dry, fruity Sancerre wines of the Loire Valley in France. In California, it is grown throughout Napa and the Central Coast. Robert Mondavi popularized Sauvignon Blanc in the 1970s by renaming it Fumé Blanc. The two names are synonymous.

The following is a complete list of vinifera varietals approved by the Bureau of Alcohol, Firearms and Tobacco for use on wine labels:

Albariño
Alicante Bouschet
Aligoté
Aramon
Arneis
Barbera
Black Corinth
Cabernet Franc
Cabernet Sauvignon
Carignan
Carmenère
Carnelian
Charbono
Chardonnay
Chenin Blanc
Cinsault
Colombard
Counoise
Duriff
Fiano
Gamay Noir
Gewürztraminer
Grenache
Grignolino
Gros Verdot
Grüner Veltliner
Kerner
Malbec
Marsanne
Melon
Merlot
Meunier
Mission
Morio-Muskat
Mourvédre/Mataro
Müller-Thurgau
Muscadelle
Muscat
Nebbiolo
Petite Sirah
Petite Verdot
Pinot Blanc
Pinot Gris
Pinot Meunier
Pinot Noir
Pinot St. George
Pinotage
Primativo
Riesling
Rousanne
Rubired

Ruby Cabernet
Sangiovese
Sauvignon Blanc
Scheurebe
Sémillon
Souzão
St. Laurent
St. Macaire
Syrah/Shiraz
Tempranillo
Terret
Tinta Barroca
Tinta Cão
Tinta Negra Mole
Valdepeñas
Valdiguié
Verdelho
Verdicchio
Vernaccia
Viognier
Zinfandel

SPECIAL CASE:
Fumé Blanc—different name but same grape as Sauvignon Blanc; the change in name has been attributed to Robert Mondavi, who in 1968 wanted to distinguish his style of making Sauvignon Blanc wines dry instead of sweet. Any winery may use the name to describe a wine made with seventy-five percent Sauvignon Blanc grapes.

Pruning, almost always done by hand, begins in the winter months (January or February) after harvest and is accomplished in such a way as to allow a maximum amount of sunshine to evenly reach all grape clusters on the vines. Winemakers keep a close eye on the progress of the grapes throughout summer, and as harvest approaches, they begin to routinely pick clusters of grapes to test sugar levels, acid levels, and the concentration of tannins. Winemakers will also chew the grapes and decide when the time is exactly right to harvest based on their own instincts, tastes, and style of winemaking. The grapes will then be harvested (in September or October) by scores of workers who work non-stop for weeks at a time, picking the grapes by hand, placing them in bins, and then transporting them to winery facilities where the wine will be made. Once transported, the grapes are de-stemmed and crushed in a large, mechanical press, and then moved into sealable plastic bins or stainless steel tanks to begin fermenting. At this point, some winemakers add cultured yeasts to the grapes' naturally occurring yeasts in order to speed up or slow down the natural rate of fermentation.

For white wine, grapes are pressed immediately after harvest and typically only the juice will be fermented. In contrast, red wine is fermented with the skins; the juice is only separated from the skins after enough color and tannins have been extracted, usually after a few days. This adds another step to red wine fermentation because the skins and seeds, which are lighter than the juice, rise to the top of fermentation bins, forming a cap that has to be regularly broken to let enough air in or the flavor, color, and texture won't be consistent. Winemakers have to regularly "punch down" the skins to keep them broken and submerged in the juice. After fermentation, the skins are pressed off and the juice is transferred to barrels.

During fermentation, wine is held in temperature-controlled (forty to eighty-six degrees Fahrenheit) tanks to allow any added yeast or other solid bits known as lees, which are actually spent yeast cells, to settle to the bottom, and then the wine is moved into oak barrels and aged. The last step is to blend wine from different barrels. Blending is an essential part of winemaking, as no two barrels are ever identical. Winemakers will pick the best barrels they can find by very carefully choosing different barrels from different coopers. They do this because each barrel has its own distinctive characteristics and flavors that will find their way into the wine. Done right, the added flavors can become the wine's signature. Barrels are only used for one or two harvests, so every year a winemaker has to figure out this equation again, which is why winemaking is truly an art.

Once the wine is blended and the flavors are just right, it will then be filtered and bottled. Wine might be aged in the bottle for weeks, months, or years depending on the varietal and style. Bottles are placed in cold (fifty-five to sixty degrees Fahrenheit) storage until release.

The date of a wine's release is entirely up to the winery. Wine changes in the bottle, so winemakers will take bottles from different cases, open them and taste them on a regular basis until they feel the time is right. For most white wines, this process will happen quickly over a couple of months. For reds, it could be months or years. Even after its release, wine continues to develop in the bottle, which is why so many Americans are turning to wine collecting as a hobby. A lot of money, time, and passion are invested in every bottle, and therefore, every glass should be enjoyed as its own unique creation.

Left: Carved casks in the barrel room at the venerable Sebastiani Vineyards in Sonoma.
Right from Top to Bottom: The steps to winemaking—grapes are harvested by hand usually in September or October, and then de-stemmed and crushed before being moved into a stainless steel tank to begin fermentation. After fermenting, the wine is moved to oak barrels to age, and then finally, it is bottled. *Opposite:* Toasting new oak barrels at the Demptos Cooperage.

Grape
TO
Glass

DECEMBER

Wine is barrel aged; some whites are stored in stainless steel tanks until the wine is ready, and then it is bottled. Wine can be aged in the bottle anywhere from a few months to several years. The amount of time is based on whether the wine is a white, which takes a few months, or a red, which can take a year or longer. Time is also based on the varietal and on the winemaker's personal style. The winemaker ultimately decides when a wine (which is constantly changing in the bottle) is ready to release by tasting it regularly. It will be released when it offers the right bouquet, or blend of flavors.

JANUARY–FEBRUARY

Vines are dormant. Pruning, usually done by hand, begins. Pruning will determine the quality and quantity of the year's harvest. Plowing is also done between the vineyard rows, though plowing occurs again intermittently throughout the year.

NOVEMBER

Vineyards hibernate and vines lose their leaves. Cover crops (mustard is particularly popular) are planted in between rows of vines to nourish the soil and ward against unwanted pests and soil erosion during rains. The cover crops are not typically harvested. Wine is moved from tanks to barrels.

MARCH–APRIL

Bud break. This is an important time to protect the vines against frost, which can destroy fragile buds, which eventually develop into grape clusters. Typically, this is also when white wines from the prior harvest are bottled.

SEPTEMBER–OCTOBER

Up daily now at the crack of dawn, winemakers continue to take grape samples from every vineyard they will harvest until grapes are at the desired sugar levels and have the right balance of sugars, tannins, and acid. Sugar levels will not increase or decrease after picking, so this determination is key, as is the winemaker's ability to figure out the tannin levels, which is strictly a matter of taste. Winemakers chew the grapes and have to innately sense the tannin level. When everything is right, harvesters then work day and night to harvest the grapes at their peak ripeness, usually over a period of three weeks. Weather can greatly impact when this happens, since a late rain or unusually high heat will affect the quality of the fruit. Grapes are crushed and the resulting juice is fermented into wine. Initial fermentation takes about 10 days.

JULY

Grapes begin to change color and start to sweeten. Vineyard managers thin out grape clusters to lower grape yields and ensure that remaining grapes are of the highest quality and concentration. Red wines from the prior harvest are moved from barrels to tanks to bottles and barrels are then cleaned and prepared for the upcoming harvest.

AUGUST

Winemakers start preparing for harvest by regularly walking their vineyards, picking grapes to test sugar levels. In the winery, they are busy cleaning and sterilizing tanks and barrels, delivering bins to the vineyards and hiring workers in anticipation of the busy weeks ahead.

4

Culinary Delights

FOOD IS AS CHERISHED AS WINE in Napa
and Sonoma, and it makes sense, since food and
wine are meant to go together. The same conditions that make the Wine Country so ideal for
growing wine grapes also work for all manner of
fresh fruit, vegetables, and for the grazing of live-
stock, dairy cows, and goats, who in turn help
produce some of the best milk, cheeses, and
creams imaginable. And thanks to the availability
of so many culinary delights, food is celebrated as
an essential part of the wine country experience.

When Copia: The American Center of Wine,
Food, and the Arts debuted in downtown Napa in
November of 2001, *The New York Times* perceptibly
said, "The good life is a religion in Northern
California. Now, it finally has a temple." And it's
true, food and wine are everything here, where
people devote their lives to producing it, consum-
ing it, and revering it. Copia occupies twelve
acres of pristine land along the Napa River, where
along with an 80,000-square-foot indoor
museum, auditoriums, and a divine restaurant
named in honor of Julia Child, the grounds
boast three-and-a-half stunning acres of
organic gardens (which supply fresh
produce to the restaurant).

Left: **California Wine Country tempts
picnickers to wile the day away in
its midst.** *Right:* **Cheese is
the perfect accompaniment
to wine.**

Much of the money behind Copia came from founders Robert and Margrit Mondavi, who gave $20 million to build it.

Another of Napa's crowning food symbols is Greystone, the Culinary Institute of America's California outpost. Greystone is a marvel in itself, a massive, romantic stone structure of epic proportion, situated on a hillside about a quarter-mile north of Main Street in St. Helena. Once upon a time, Greystone belonged to the Christian Brothers Winery, which bought it in 1950. Christian Brothers started making wine as far back as 1879 and stayed solvent during Prohibition selling wine for sacramental use. A century later, brandy made up eighty percent of the company's revenues, and when Christian Brothers was bought by international distributor Heublien in 1989 for $200 million, it was the largest winery sale in U.S. history.

CIA, as the Culinary Institute of America is called, first opened in 1946 as the New Haven Restaurant Institute in New Haven, CT, with fifty students. The flagship school is now based in Hyde Park, New York and is the only culinary institute to administer the American Culinary Federation's master chef exam. Greystone is the institute's continuing education wing, where professionals can

update their skills and knowledge. It also offers an advanced culinary arts certificate program, a baking and pastry chef certificate program, and features a 15,000-square-foot teaching area. For the public, it offers an adult career discovery program for those thinking about becoming a chef, as well as a myriad of wine programs, cooking demonstrations, and special events. An on-site bakery/cafe and food-focused marketplace, which includes one of the best cookbook shops around, are open daily.

The building itself was built in the 1880s when it became the largest stone winery in the world, with a capacity of close to 2 million gallons. It encompasses 117,000-square-feet, has twenty-two-inch thick walls and was designed by the same Hammond McIntyre behind the wineries at Far Niente, Inglenook (now Francis Ford Coppola's Niebaum-Coppola), and Trefethen. It was originally utilized as a cooperative for local growers to come crush their grapes and store their wine.

Top: **Margrit and Robert Mondavi's Copia, a temple to wine, food, and the arts.** *Left:* **The restaurant at Copia, Julia's Kitchen, was named after the famous Julia Child.** *Bottom:* **Chefs at work at Greystone in St. Helena, the Culinary Institute of America's west coast location.** *Opposite:* **Greystone was built in the 1880s, and at that time, it was the largest stone winery in the world.**

Frenchman Charles Carpy bought it in 1894 to house the California Wine Association, which exerted considerable influence on the price and quality of California wine for decades. But by the time the Christian Brothers took it over, Greystone had suffered years of neglect. In the end, Heublien generously donated the place to the CIA, which only had to come up with $1.8 million to buy the $14 million property, and after a $15-million retrofit in 1995, Greystone once again opened its huge redwood entrance doors.

Most people visit the building's signature restaurant, which goes out of its way to highlight local wines and microbrews. Every table has a view of the chefs at work. And unlike other cooking schools, the chefs are not students. Chef de Cuisine Pilar Sanchez is a California native who hosts her own Food Network show called *Melting Pot*. Meals begin with a plate of small "temptations" assembled with local ingredients, and a glass of Greystone's exclusive sparkling Querenica Brut Rosé. The wine list is four pages long.

While Greystone is part-architecture and part-cuisine, Yountville's French Laundry is all about the food. Consistently hailed as one of the top five restaurants in America (it is number one on a lot of people's lists), food connoisseurs dream about this type of experience all their lives. As a result, Chef/Owner Thomas Keller, who has won just about every cooking award in existence, requires that reservations for his sixty-two-seat dining room be made two months in advance. A turn-of-the-century two-story building built as a French steam laundry, Keller bought the restaurant in 1994 with the dream of creating a three-star country French restaurant. He has created that and more—a masterpiece.

Also in Yountville, Domaine Chandon, owned by Moët-Hennessy of Dom Pérignon fame, invites diners to pair the winery's own sparkling wines with four-star seasonal menu choices, all in view of the Carneros Valley.

In Napa town, a restaurant resurgence is in full swing, and among the eateries leading the way is Cole's Chop House, a classic steak house on two levels with a lengthy wine list full of delicious reds. Chef Greg Cole also owns Celadon, a purveyor of "global comfort food," located just a few blocks south. Zu Zu is a fun new addition to Main Street and offers a tempting selection of tapas.

Top: The French-style gardens of Thomas Keller's French Laundry in Yountville, arguably the best restaurant in America. *Above:* Gourmet pizza and a glass of bubbly at Domaine Chandon. *Bottom:* Just one of the many delights offered through Chef Keller's unique menu.

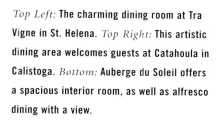

Top Left: The charming dining room at Tra Vigne in St. Helena. *Top Right:* This artistic dining area welcomes guests at Catahoula in Calistoga. *Bottom:* Auberge du Soleil offers a spacious interior room, as well as alfresco dining with a view.

For a more classic experience, Bistro Don Giovanni set back from the St. Helena Highway, blends California, French, and Italian influences in a fancier setting. Up the highway is another standby, Brix, which tends its own organic garden.

Rutherford's out-of-the-way gem is Auberge du Soleil, a sophisticated restaurant and overnight spa. Its dining room opens onto an inviting terrace with birds' eye views of the Valley. In St. Helena, in addition to Greystone, serious eaters flock to Tra Vigne for Italian food or to the Martini House to enjoy "Napa Cuisine" made from local produce and farm-raised meat and poultry.

Farther up the valley, Calistoga has a handful of superior restaurants within walking distance of one another. One favorite is The Catahoula Restaurant & Saloon, situated in the historic Mount View Hotel on Calistoga's main drag. Around since 1994, the restaurant, which specializes in southern cooking, is named after the official dog of Louisiana. A native of Baton Rouge, Chef Jan Birnbaum once served as an assistant to Paul Prudhomme. The restaurant features a wood-burning oven, poolside seating in good weather, and a light-hearted sense of food as fun. Around the corner a couple blocks, Wappo Bar & Bistro has tables under a beautiful grapevine arbor and features cuisines from around the world with a local twist.

Finding the Perfect Match

Much is written about the pairing of food and wine, and while there seem to be a lot of rules, the truth is it is best not to limit yourself. Every wine is made differently, even within varietals, and everybody's tastes are different so experimentation is the key.

It helps to know that wine is described as having six basic characteristics: acidity, bitterness, oak, saltiness, sweetness, and alcohol. A fine wine manages to balance all six characteristics. How wine matches up with food literally has to do with the chemical reactions that occur when different components come together. A perfect example of this is the tried-and-true way red meat pairs well with the tannins in red wine, or the way fish is nice with white varietals. So what is the general rule? Lighter bodied wines are better with lighter ingredients, while heavier wines are best with heavier foods. Below are six of the most commonly found wines and their usual characteristics, ordered from lightest to heaviest.

SAUVIGNON BLANC
Sauvignon Blanc is a white wine typically higher in acid and light in oak, as it rarely sees time in oak barrels. Wines high in acidity amplify the subtle flavors of food and cleanse the palate in between rich or oily foods. It often has grassy, citrus aromas and is described as tasting refreshing, crisp, cool, clean, and aromatic. A light wine, it is often enjoyed without food but also pairs well with light dishes, such as hors d'oeuvres like cheeses, deli meats, deviled eggs, asparagus, artichokes, smoked salmon, and spinach dips. It also goes well with shellfish (which often are covered in lemon, pairing citrus with citrus), salmon, and seafood pastas.

CHARDONNAY
Chardonnay is a white wine higher in alcohol than Sauvignon Blanc and is considered fuller bodied and more aromatic. This wine can vary in acid levels (California vintages are usually lower in acid, while French ones are higher) and almost always spends time in oak barrels, but for varying lengths of time. The barrel wood can contribute distinctive toast, caramel, and vanilla flavors. As a result, wine tasters often describe Chardonnay as buttery, creamy, vanilla-flavored, and spicy. It also picks up hints of tropical fruit flavors such as apple, pear, peaches, apricots, and nectarines. The wine pairs very well with a lot of dishes, including chicken, turkey, pork, and fish dishes, and is a favorite with Dungeness crab and grilled salmon. It also pairs nicely with creamy pastas, salads, French onion soup, and clam chowder. For dessert, it is a good accompaniment to apple tarts, pies, custards, and crème brûlée.

PINOT NOIR
Pinot Noir is aromatic, elegant, smooth, and delicate, and it is considered the most versatile of all reds in terms of pairing with food. It almost always sees oak barrels. People often taste wild berries in Pinot Noir, and it goes well with everything from shellfish to steak to game. The wine's spicy elements can bring out the flavors in grilled meats, while rich, acidic Pinots would be a wise choice with savory or sweet soufflés, omelets, crepes, Asian fare, or lasagna. As for desserts, a meringue, angel cake, or sponge cake would be the right match.

MERLOT
Merlot is a robust grape that has more body than Pinot Noir, and it has a moderate exposure to oak barrels while aging. The wine is spicy, dark, and rich with hints of blueberry, blackberry, and cinnamon. A good Merlot will have the perfect balance between acid, fruit, and tannins. It is quite simply the quintessential middle-of-the-road option, which is also why it is often used to tone down fuller bodied grape varietals like Cabernet Sauvignon. On its own, it can stand up to red meats and be a good mate to poultry, fish, berry desserts, and cheesecakes.

ZINFANDEL
Zinfandel is a dark rich wine often described as being all spice and fruit, making it both spicy and sweet. It is usually lower in acid, but heavy on oak, alcohol, and tannins, giving it a substantial bite when drunk without food. Tannins, which are present in grape skins, seeds, and the oak barrels used for aging, contribute a certain amount of bitterness, so wines high in tannins go well with dishes featuring naturally bitter ingredients. They also balance out fatty, rich foods like cheese. Oddly enough, being the only true American varietal, Zinfandel goes amazingly

well with traditional American fare such as hamburgers, pizza, and chili, as well as with Mexican, Indian, and Thai dishes. A ginger spice cake or any kind of chocolate concoction enjoyed with a good Zinfandel will turn the meal into a taste sensation.

CABERNET SAUVIGNON
Cabernet Sauvignon is a big red described as tasting like mocha, chocolate, anise, and blackberries. Heavy in oak, Cabernet Sauvignons go best with big meats—steak, lamb, BBQ, spicy or blackened chicken—and rich chocolate desserts.

SYRAH
Syrah is bigger than Cabernet Sauvignon in many people's minds, though there is not total agreement on that classification. Syrah is spicy, sweet, peppery, rich, dark, thick, fruity, and can be summed up with one word—intense. High in alcohol with a fair amount of acid, it goes well with spicy, fruity dishes, fatty cheeses, dark red meats, spicy Asian dishes, grilled food, stews, casseroles, and heavy custards. It is also an ideal wine for hearty, wintertime foods.

Opposite: A simple glass of white wine can complement a wide variety of foods. *Left:* Braised rabbit and asparagus from Tra Vigne. *Top:* An artfully arranged entrée from Robert Mondavi Winery. *Above:* John Ash and Co.'s espresso brownie torte.

No visit to the Valley should go without a stop at the Oakville Grocery, a packed deli and grocery for committed gastronomists. Dean & DeLuca, a more recent addition to St. Helena, is another haven for food hedonists.

As one of the state's most diverse agricultural landscapes, Sonoma easily rivals Napa for Wine Country cuisine dominance, with Healdsburg the beating heart of Sonoma's extended food body.

Healdsburg has always been a hub for can't miss restaurants, but the addition of Dry Creek Kitchen to the town's charming central square, has substantially sealed the deal. The centerpiece of the luxurious Hotel Healdsburg, Dry Creek Kitchen was opened in 2001 by famed chef Charlie Palmer of New York City's Aureole. Palmer's Kitchen relies on fresh produce and gourmet food purveyors to assemble its signature meals. The restaurant also takes pride in its great list of Sonoma County wines, many of which are in limited production. The outdoor terrace on the square is a particularly good place to sit. Manzanita, Ravenous, and Zin are also worthy options just off the square.

Tucked away off River Road in Santa Rosa within the Vintners' Inn, John Ash & Co. is the namesake restaurant of resident chef, educator, and author John Ash, who over twenty years has become a big name in the Wine Country food world. His book *From Earth to the Table* won the Julia Child Award for Best American Cookbook. Ash teaches at Greystone and is also the culinary director at Fetzer Vineyards in Mendocino County.

Top: A favorite stop in St. Helena is the Oakville Grocery, where you can pack up your picnic basket with fresh produce and deli items. *Middle:* Indulge in a warm duck breast salad from John Ash & Co. *Bottom:* A wealth of culinary choices await at Dean & DeLuca.

The town of Sonoma has a few culinary aces up its sleeve, including The General's Daughter, a grand Victorian tribute to Natalia Vallejo, who was General Mariano Vallejo's daughter. Since 1994, it has existed to serve locally inspired meals in a warm setting, just three blocks from the Sonoma Square. Often seen on "Best Of" lists, tiny Café La Haye, just off the square, serves "California-eclectic" cuisine. Also in Sonoma, The Girl & The Fig highlights California-style country cooking and emphasizes Rhone varietals like Syrah, Grenache, and Viognier on its wine list. Up the Valley in Glen Ellen, sister restaurant The Girl & The Gaucho is a tapas place, next door to the superb Glen Ellen Inn & Restaurant. And just up the road, Saffron is

Top: **California's wine region offers endless amounts of fresh cheese, meat, and dairy due to its lush green pastures.**

quickly becoming a must-stop destination for those who love its romantically-lit outdoor terrace and classic California cuisine.

One of Sonoma County's biggest gifts to the community is Farm Trails, an organization that serves to promote agricultural diversity by bringing to light a variety of independent, local providers of fresh vegetables, berries, cheeses, meats, wines, plants, flowers, and much more. Signs are posted wherever a farmer sells directly to the public, and the experience of visiting these ranches and farms can be as enjoyable as the tasty purchases you take

home. Among the members is family-run Vella Cheese Company, which has been making fresh and dry Jack cheeses from Sonoma grass-fed cows since 1931.

It is no accident that nature put food and wine together in this amazing region of California. Luther Burbank, the noted farmer who came to Santa Rosa in 1875, once wrote about this lush, fertile region, "This is the chosen spot of all this earth as far as Nature is concerned." And it remains today the chosen spot for all who love to celebrate the good life.

5

Traditions & Celebrations

THE CALIFORNIA WINE COUNTRY is a gourmand's playground, a physically beautiful piece of earth inextricably wrapped in all the elements of the good life. And because of this, there are numerous traditions that have sprung up over the years to celebrate the hard work and good fortune that goes into Wine Country living.

The Napa Valley Mustard Festival heralds the arrival of wild mustard across the vineyards each winter. Francisco Junipero Serra is credited with bringing mustard to Northern California and it thrives here, turning great expanses of the land a stunning yellow. Grape growers love it as a cover crop, effective as it is against soil erosion. Vineyard managers also plow it into the ground and it becomes a natural fertilizer. Mustard season, which is January through March, now attracts twenty-seven percent of the Valley's visitors every year, and the annual festival features a dozen events that pay homage to the beauty and ecology of wild mustard.

Left: **Large trees offer shade over the beautiful vineyards of California's Wine Country.** *Right:* **Taking a hot air balloon tour over the Napa Valley is a relaxing way to appreciate its beauty from above.**

While Napa celebrates mustard, Sonoma exalts the olive. The Sonoma Valley Olive Festival is another three-month long winter celebration, full of feasts, tastings, olive oil workshops, and even a "Blessing of the Olives," which is a mandatory tradition that takes place at the Sonoma Mission. All things olive, especially oil, saw a revival in the Valley in 1993 after winemaker B.R. Cohn released an olive oil made from trees that had been planted in the 1870s on his winery's estate in Glen Ellen. His renewed interest and success opened the doors for others to follow.

Many people come to the Wine Country to unwind and be pampered, and there are a handful of first-rate luxury spas ready to accommodate those in need of a relaxing soak. The Spa at Silverado Country Club & Resort in Napa is a new addition to the Valley and is already raising the bar for what a spa experience should be. Silverado, built in the 1870s by General John F. Miller, was originally part of Salvador (brother to General) Vallejo's ranch, and at 16,000-square-feet it is the biggest resort in the Napa Valley. The 1200-acre spread features two 18-hole golf courses that wrap around the estate's historic mansion. Meadowood is another amazing place to sequester, with a health spa, wine center, and comfortable cottages set against forested hillsides and dreamy gardens. Its grassy meadows are perfect for games of croquet. The resort, which lies off the Silverado Trail in St. Helena, also offers a 2014-yard, 9-hole golf course. Or, for the day, try any of the numerous spas based in Calistoga, home to natural mineral waters and mud baths.

In Sonoma, there is the signature adobe-style Sonoma Mission Inn & Spa, which became part of the Fairmont's offerings in 2002. Set just above the town of Sonoma, the Mission Inn is one of the area's first resorts and offers visitors a 40,000-square foot spa based on natural thermal waters that flow from below the Inn. The secluded 18-hole golf course dates back to 1927.

Over 100,000 people annually ride the Napa Wine Train, a restored Southern Pacific line that meanders at twenty mph or less through the Napa Valley starting from the town of Napa, through the vineyards of Yountville, Oakville, and Rutherford, turning around just past St. Helena. Three-hour brunch, lunch, and dinner excursions are available, as are private tours and tastings at specific wineries featured along the way.

Top: One of two golf courses that sprawl across the 1200-acre Silverado Country Club in Napa. *Above:* An old-fashioned game of croquet is the ideal way to spend the day enjoying Meadowood's pristine greens. *Below:* The Napa Wine Train meanders through the vines. *Opposite:* Take in the quiet woods and trickling waters of Robert Louis Stevenson State Park.

IN HONOR OF
Jack London

Jack London was born in 1876 and achieved international acclaim in 1903 for his novel *Call of the Wild.* Born in San Francisco, London met his second wife, Charmian Kittredge, in Glen Ellen, where her family had extensive land holdings. After serving as a war correspondent in the Russian-Japanese war and traveling through the South Pacific by boat, the intrepid adventurer settled down in Sonoma in 1909, where he bought land and reached the peak of his career, bringing Glen Ellen its own brush with fame with the 1913 novel *Valley of the Moon.* The Londons spent the next several years experimenting with agriculture and building a massive stone house called "Wolf House." But a mysterious fire destroyed the house before they even moved in, and London died three years later from gastrointestinal poisoning. He was only forty.

Decades later, London's nephew, Irving Shepard, donated 40 acres to the state and a park was born. It has since grown to include London's grave, the Wolf House ruins, and Charmian's House of Happy Walls, built in 1919 to contain London's personal collection of a life of travels. Today, the park includes over 800 acres of trails. The vineyards on London's estate belong to Chateau St. Jean, which is just up the road in Kenwood. Every year they make a special wine in his honor.

Top: Author Jack London's study.
Right: The ruins of Wolf House, the house that Jack built but never enjoyed.

If seeing vineyards from the air is more your cup of tea, Sonoma's Vintage Aircraft Company can provide a scenic flight in a 1940 Boeing biplane or authentic Navy Warbird. "Aerobatic" and "Kamikaze" options include loops, rolls, and other trick maneuvers. Balloons Above The Valley, one of several area balloon operators, will transport you high above the vineyards at a much slower pace, complete with a champagne brunch upon landing. Bike rentals and other adventure excursions are available throughout Wine Country as well.

For hiking, the North Bay's highest peak, 4,344-foot Mt. St. Helena, officially a part of Robert Louis Stevenson State Park, challenges visitors with some awesome trail climbs. From the trailhead off of Highway 29 in Calistoga, it's a ten-mile, 2,000-foot elevation gain, roundtrip hike to the summit, which offers exquisite views of the entire Napa Valley and beyond. Or, wander the woods of Jack London State Historic Park, just outside of Glen Ellen. The celebrated author bought 127 acres here in 1905 and later built the Wolf House, which tragically burnt down the night before London and his wife Charmian were to move in. An easy trail leads to the Wolf House ruins. A path to the top of Sonoma Mountain also ascends from the park's visitor center.

There are so many wineries to visit throughout Napa and Sonoma that it would be impossible to list all the virtues of each, but a few definitely stand out for their historic or artistic significance, their intense beauty, or their ability to offer something slightly different. In Calistoga, Chateau Montelena is where the modern Napa legend kicked off. It was this winery's 1973 Chardonnay that took the world by surprise by winning the 1976 blind taste test in Paris. In addition to its wines, the facility offers a beautiful mini lake, where arched bridges lead to cozy islands ideal for picnicking. Also in Calistoga, Sterling Vineyards is on a small hilltop and can only be visited by taking a tram up to unrivaled views of the vineyards below. At Calistoga's Clos Pegase, a significant art collection is on display within 21,000 square feet of caves. Beringer Vineyards, on Main Street in St. Helena, is the oldest continuously operating winery in the Napa Valley and a stunning spot for a picnic or a mid-afternoon stroll. Built in 1876, the winery features a series of tunnels dug into the hillside used as naturally temperature-controlled aging cellars. Also not to be missed is the Robert Mondavi Winery in Oakville, a stoic Mission-style building as grand as its owner.

Top: The serene lake at Chateau Montelena is the ideal place to contemplate the world.

Above: A sky-high gondola makes its way to Sterling Vineyards.

Opposite: Beringer's Rhine House was built by Frederick Beringer in 1883 and is on the National Register of Historic Places. The winery is one of the oldest in the Valley.

Pages 52-53: Brilliantly colored poppies grow wild throughout the Valley of the Moon.

Along the Silverado Trail, Robert Sinskey Vineyards, a lesser-known Pinot Noir producer, always has a first-rate chef in residence, whipping up appetizers to go with whatever wine is being poured that day. Or, step back into the Napa of centuries ago at Niebaum-Coppola in Rutherford. Owned by esteemed filmmaker Francis Ford Coppola, the romantic ivy-covered stone estate was once home to Inglenook. Winemaker Gustave Niebaum purchased the property in 1879 and built the Gothic winery in 1886. Inglenook wines reappeared after Prohibition under the guidance of John Daniel, Jr., a distant relative, who ran the brand during its glory years, from 1936 until 1964,

when the winery was sold. Coppola started buying different sections of the original Niebaum estate in 1974. Also in Rutherford, Beaulieu Vineyard offers a glimpse at the past, where noted enologist André Tchelistcheff made legendary Cabernets and Chardonnays under the direction of winery founder Georges de Latour.

If art is your passion, there are several wineries that showcase extensive art collections. The Hess Collection and Winery in the town of Napa is well known for its private modern art collection, while the di Rosa Preserve in Carneros is actually the vision of a winemaker who sacrificed wine for art, when Rene di Rosa's coveted Winery Lake Vineyards was sold to Seagram in 1986. After the sale, Rene and wife Veronica kept enough land to showcase twentieth-century Bay Area art over a beautiful 200 acres.

Top Left: A stained-glass window peers out to the vineyards from Niebaum-Coppola.
Top Right: Once home to Inglenook, the ivy-covered Niebaum-Coppola is one of the most beautiful wineries in Napa Valley.
Left: A car from Francis Ford Coppola's Tucker is on display at the winery.

1} Start by holding up the glass and looking at the color. White wines range in color from clear to honey-colored to gold. Younger ones can almost look green, while older ones turn golden-brown with age. Younger red wines will be shades of red and purple. Older reds will look brick red or reddish-brown. If a wine is cloudy, it contains sediment and should be decanted before it is served.

SEE

2} The general consensus among experts is that eighty percent of a wine's taste is in its smell. The way to release a wine's aromas, also known as its bouquet, is to swirl the glass. Wine glasses are tapered slightly at the top in order to capture the bouquet after swirling. The "legs" that run down the inside of the glass can be a barometer of the wine's alcohol content. If the wine is thick and runs down slowly, it has a high alcohol content; if it is thin and runs quickly, the wine has a low alcohol content.

SWIRL

3} After swirling the wine, focus on the bouquet. You should be able to smell fruit or maybe even oak, depending on how long the wine spent fermenting in barrels. Try to identify what type of fruit you can smell. White wines often smell like apples, pears, apricots, peaches, citrus, or even fresh vegetables or flowers. Reds can smell like cherries, raspberries, blackberries, and currants, or like chocolate, tobacco, spices, flowers, or even leather. If a wine smells like vinegar or cork, there is usually something wrong.

SMELL

The **6** *Stages of Wine Tasting*

SIP

4} Next, take a small sip and let the wine slowly coat your tongue. Different parts of the tongue pick up different flavors. Hold the wine in your mouth and inhale to aerate it. By doing so, you will be able to detect more of the fruit tastes and to sense whether it is light or full-bodied, bitter or sweet. It is often a good idea to taste wine with food. For example, a bite of cheese will help smooth out the tannins in red wine. And if a wine doesn't taste right to you on the first try, taste it again as the first sip is not always reliable.

SAVOR

5} If you will be tasting multiple wines, spit each wine out after trying it. After you do, see how long the flavors linger. The mark of a well-made wine is its finish and the way its flavors continue to reveal themselves. The taste will dissipate more quickly in a lower quality wine.

SUMMARIZE

6} What did the wine taste like? Does it have a nice aftertaste? Rinse the glass and taste something else. Keep notes of what elements you liked so that you will have a better understanding of your tastes in the future.

Art & Architecture

The Wine Country offers an architectural feast for the eyes, where individual styles blend seamlessly among the rows of vines. In some cases, the buildings reflect the vines in terms of quality and complexity. In other cases, the buildings are destinations in themselves.

1.) Sterling Vineyards clean white look, modeled after the Greek architecture on Mykonos, is a crisp contrast to the greenery of its surroundings. 2.) Spring Mountain Winery was once the setting for the popular television series Falcon Crest about a fictional winemaking family in Napa Valley, though only the exterior was used. It is closed to the public, but loyal watchers of the show often try to get a glimpse of the interior. 3.) Hop Kiln in the Russian River Valley was indeed used as a place to dry hops, once an important industry in the area. Built in 1905, it is one of California's Historic Landmarks. 4.) Monticello's "Jefferson House" was styled after the former president's Virginia estate. 5.) The ostentatious Ledson Winery occupies 16,000 square feet of prime Sonoma Valley land and is meant to be a French-Normandy castle. Designed by the Ledson family, the brick edifice comes complete with seven fireplaces. 6.) Chateau Boswell could double for a castle along the Loire. 7.) The massive stone, ivy-covered V. Sattui Winery looks like an Italian monastery and dates back to 1885. 8.) St. Clement's Gothic-Victorian Rosenbaum House first became a winery in 1878 and features a maze of stone cellars beneath. 9.) Stately Clos Pegase was named after the mythical horse Pegasus and was designed by renowned architect Michael Graves. It has 20,000 feet of caves for aging and is as much an art museum as a winery.

3

5

7

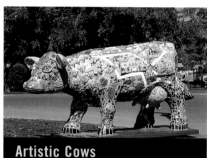

Artistic Cows

COWS! is a public art project designed to raise awareness and funds for arts programs in Sonoma Valley. In November 2000, over sixty local artists started painting round resin cows that were then displayed throughout Sonoma County. Each cow was sponsored by an individual or business and then auctioned off to the public in August, 2002. The cows, including everything from the "Senorita Delfina, La Vaca from Oaxaca" to a cork-covered cow named "Phellos" (Greek for cork), were on display at Ravenswood Winery. Similar to successful COWS! programs in Zurich, Toronto, Chicago, and New York, the Sonoma program differed in that it did not rely on municipal funding, but instead involved local artists and farmers on a more personal level. Over $150,000 was raised. Some cows can still be seen throughout the Valley and photos of the cows exist on www.sonomacows.com.

Carneros is also where you'll find majestic Domaine Carneros, established in 1989 by Claude Taittinger of the French Taittinger Champagne house so that he could make sparkling wine in Napa. Taittinger spent $9 million building the eighteenth-century, Louis XV-style chateau set on a hill overlooking his vineyards, a replica of his family's castle in France. The chateau is a stunning work of art in its own right.

Also in Carneros is Gloria Ferrer Champagne Caves. Originally from Spain, the Ferrer family has been making sparkling wine for over a century. The terrace from their Sonoma location provides one of the best views of the Carneros Valley. Closer to the Sonoma Square, Gundlach-Bundschu makes for a relaxed visit—the winery's entire philosophy revolves around making wine fun. They offer guided tours, movie nights, and a midsummer Mozart festival. Thirty-something President and CEO Jeff Bundschu is responsible for a group called the Wine Brats, which actively preaches the joy of not taking wine too seriously.

For wine historians, two places of interest are the Buena Vista Winery, which helped launch the Northern California wine industry, and Sebastiani Vineyards, where Franciscan monks planted vines in 1825. Further up the Valley in Glen Ellen, the Benziger family takes visitors through its vineyards by tram, stopping to appreciate each vine, while Chateau St. Jean, known for its spectacular Chardonnay and Cabernet Sauvignon wines,

offers up a stunning 1920s chateau, fish ponds, and formal estate gardens perfect for a summer picnic.

Napa and Sonoma are famous for their wine, but that is not the only appeal. The historic festivals, the venerated spas and resorts, the awe-inspiring landscapes, and the timeless traditions are all a part of the good life that is celebrated in California's Wine Country.

Opposite: **Chateau St. Jean's courtside gardens surround the winery's 1920 chateau, where exceptional Chardonnays are made.** *Left:* **One of Sonoma's artistic cows.** *Top and Above:* **The view from Domaine Carneros' $9 million chateau, which is seen above.**

A PARTIAL LIST OF
The Wineries

⊙ Open to the public, please call for hours.

☎ Open to the public by appointment only, please call ahead.

✖ Closed to the public.

Acacia
2750 Las Amigas Road, Napa
707-226-9991 ⊙

Armida Winery
2201 Westside Road, Healdsburg
707-433-2222 ⊙
www.armida.com

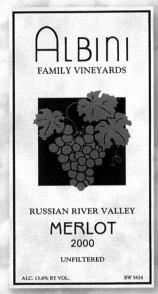

Albini Family Vineyards
886 Jensen Lane, Windsor
707-838-9249 ☎

Arrowood Winery
14347 Sonoma Hwy, Glen Ellen
707-935-2600 ☎
www.arrowoodvineyards.com

Artesa Winery
1345 Henry Road, Napa
707-224-1668 ⊙
www.artesawinery.com

Alderbrook Vineyards & Winery
2306 Magnolia Drive, Healdsburg
707-433-5987 ⊙
www.alderbrook.com

Adler Fels Winery
5325 Corrick Road, Santa Rosa
707-539-3123 ☎
www.adlerfelswinery.com

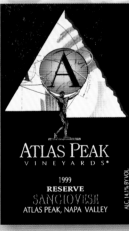

Atlas Peak Vineyards
3700 Soda Canyon Road, Napa
707-252-7971 ✖

Ballentine
2820 St. Helena Hwy, St. Helena
707-963-7919 ☎

Barnett Vineyards
4070 Spring Mountain Road, St. Helena
707-963-7075 ☎

Battaglini Estate Winery
2948 Piner Road, Santa Rosa
707-578-4091 ☎
www.battagliniwines.com

Beaucanon Estate
1006 Monticello Road, Napa
707-967-3520 ⊙

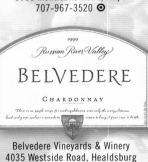

Belvedere Vineyards & Winery
4035 Westside Road, Healdsburg
707-431-4442 ⊙

Beaulieu Vineyard
1960 St. Helena Hwy, Rutherford
707-967-5230 ⊙
www.bvwine.com

Benziger Family Winery
1883 London Ranch Road, Glen Ellen
707-935-3000 ⊙

Beringer Vineyards
2000 Main Street, St. Helena
707-963-4812 ⊙

Blackstone Winery
8450 Sonoma Hwy, Kenwood
707-833-1999 ⊙
www.blackstonewinery.com

Bouchaine Vineyards
1075 Buchli and Station Road, Napa
707-252-9065 ⊙

Benessere
1010 Big Tree Road, St. Helena
707-963-5853 ☎

Buena Vista Winery
18000 Old Winery Road, Sonoma
707-938-1266 ⊙
www.buenavistawinery.com

Cain Vineyard & Winery
3800 Langtry Road, St. Helena
707-963-1616 ☎

Cakebread Cellars
8300 St. Helena Hwy, Rutherford
707-963-5221 ⊙

⊙ Open to the public, please call for hours.   ☎ Open to the public by appointment only, please call ahead.   ✖ Closed to the public.

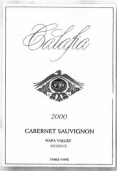

Calafia Cellars
629 Fulton Lane, St. Helena
707-963-0114 ☎

Chappellet Winery and Vineyard
1581 Sage Canyon Road, St. Helena
707-963-7136 ◉

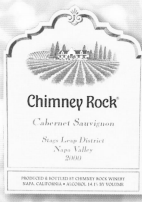

Chimney Rock Winery
5350 Silverado Trail, Napa
707-257-2641 ◉

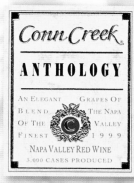

Conn Creek Winery/Villa Mt. Eden
8711 Silverado Trail, St. Helena
707-963-9100 ◉

Cuvaison
4550 Silverado Trail, Calistoga
707-942-6266 ◉

Casa Nuestra
3451 Silverado Trail, St. Helena
707-963-5783 ◉
www.casanuestra.com

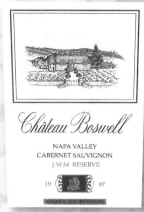

Chateau Boswell
3468 Silverado Trail, St. Helena
707-963-5472 ☎

Cline Cellars
24737 Hwy 121, Sonoma
707-940-4030 ◉
www.clinecellars.com

Constant-Diamond Mountain Vineyards
2121 Diamond Mountain Road, Calistoga
707-942-0707 ☎

Dalla Valle Vineyards
7776 Silverado Trail, Oakville
707-944-2676 ✖

Castle Vineyards
1105 Castle Road, Sonoma
707-996-4188 ☎
www.castlevineyards.com

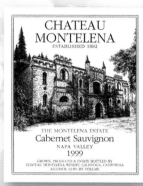

Chateau Montelena Winery
1429 Tubbs Lane, Calistoga
707-942-5105 ◉

Clos du Val
5330 Silverado Trail, Napa
707-259-2225 ◉
www.closduval.com

Corison Winery
987 South St. Helena Hwy, St. Helena
707-963-0826 ☎

Darioush Winery
4240 Silverado Trail, Napa
707-257-2345 ◉

Catacula Lake Winery
4105 Chiles Pope Valley Road,
St. Helena
707-965-1104 ☎

Clos du Bois
19410 Geyserville Avenue, Geyserville
707-857-3100 ◉
www.closdubois.com

Cosentino Winery
7415 St. Helena Hwy, Yountville
707-944-1220 ◉

Chandelle of Sonoma
15499 Arnold Drive, Glen Ellen
800-544-8890 ◉

Chateau Potelle Winery
3875 Mount Veeder Road, Napa
707-255-9440 ◉
www.chateaupotelle.com

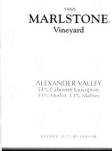

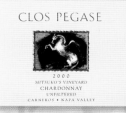

Clos Pegase
1060 Dunaweal Lane, Calistoga
707-942-4981 ◉

Crichton Hall Vineyard
1150 Darms Lane, Napa
707-224-4200 ◉

Davis Bynum Winery
8075 Westside Road, Healdsburg
707-433-5852 ◉
www.davisbynum.com

◉ Open to the public, please call for hours.   ☎ Open to the public by appointment only, please call ahead.   ✖ Closed to the public.

De Loach Vineyards
1791 Olivet Road, Santa Rosa
707-526-9111 ☉
www.deloachvineyards.com

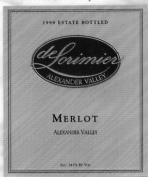

de Lorimier Winery
2001 Hwy 128, Geyserville
707-857-2000 ☉
www.delorimierwinery.com

Domaine Carneros
1240 Duhig Road, Napa
707-257-0101 ☉
www.domainecarneros.com

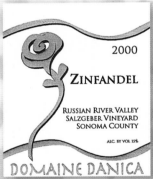

Domaine Danica
1960 Dry Creek Road, Healdsburg
707-573-1141 ☎
www.domainedanica.com

Domaine Charbay Distillery
4001 Spring Mountain Road, St. Helena
707-963-9327 ☎

Don Sebastiani & Sons
PO Box 1887, Sonoma
707-996-8463 ☎

Dry Creek Vineyard
3770 Lambert Bridge Road, Healdsburg
707-433-1000 ☉
www.drycreekvineyard.com

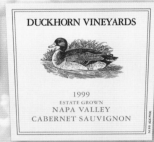

Duckhorn Vineyards
1000 Lodi Lane, St. Helena
707-963-7108 ☉

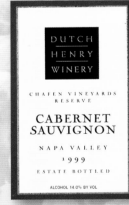

Dutch Henry Winery
4310 Silverado Trail, Calistoga
707-942-5771 ☉
www.dutchhenry.com

Edgewood Estate
401 St. Helena Hwy, St. Helena
707-963-7293 ☉

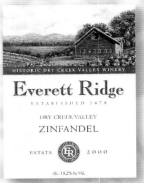

Everett Ridge Vineyards & Winery
435 West Dry Creek Road, Healdsburg
707-433-1637 ☎
www.everettridge.com

Favero Vineyards & Winery
3939 Lovall Valley Road, Sonoma
707-935-3939 ☉
www.faverovineyards.com

Ferrari-Carano Vineyards and Winery
8761 Dry Creek Road, Healdsburg
707-433-6700 ☉
www.Ferrari-carano.com

Fife Vineyards
3646 Spring Mountain Road, St. Helena
707-963-1534 ✖

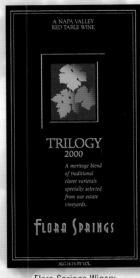

Flora Springs Winery
677 South St. Helena Hwy, St. Helena
800-913-1118 ☉
www.florasprings.com

Folie à Deux Winery
3070 North St. Helena Hwy, St. Helena
707-963-1160 ☉

Franus Wine Company
2055 Hoffman Lane, Napa
707-945-0542 ☎

Freemark Abbey Winery
3022 N. St. Helena Hwy, St. Helena
707-963-9694 ☉
www.freemarkabbey.com

Frick Winery
23072 Walling Road, Geyserville
707-857-3205 ☎
www.frickwinery.com

Franciscan Oakville Estate
Mt. Veeder Winery
1178 Galleron Road, Rutherford
707-963-7111 ☉

Fritz Winery
24691 Dutcher Creek Road, Cloverdale
707-894-3389 ☉
www.fritzwinery.com

Galleron Signature Wines
PO Box 2, Rutherford
707-265-6552 ☉

Gallo of Sonoma Tasting Room
320 Center Street, Healdsburg
707-433-2458 ⊙
www.gallo.com

Green and Red Vineyard
3208 Chiles Valley Road, St. Helena
707-965-2346 ☎

Gundlach Bundschu Winery
2000 Denmark Street, Sonoma
707-938-5277 ⊙
www.gunbun.com

Hartwell Vineyards
5795 Silverado Trail, Napa
707-255-4269 ✖

Homewood Winery
23120 Burndale Road, Sonoma
707-996-6353 ⊙

Geyser Peak Winery
2281 Chianti Road, Geyserville
707-857-9463 ⊙
www.geyserpeakwinery.com

Havens Wine Cellars
2055 Hoffman Lane, Napa
707-261-2000 ⊙

Honig Vineyard & Winery
850 Rutherford Road, Rutherford
707-963-5618 ⊙

Gloria Ferrer Champagne Caves
23555 Hwy 121, Schellville
707-996-7256 ⊙
www.gloriaferrer.com

Grgich Hills Cellars
1829 St. Helena Hwy, Rutherford
707-963-2784 ⊙
www.grgich.com

Gustavo Thrace Winery
880 Vallejo Street, Napa
707-257-6796 ☎

Heitz Wine Cellars
500 Taplin Road, St. Helena
707-963-3542 ⊙

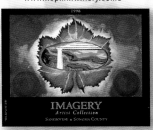

Hop Kiln Winery
6050 Westside Road, Healdsburg
707-433-6491 ⊙
www.hopkilnwinery.coms

Goosecross Cellars
1119 State Lane, Yountville
707-944-1986 ⊙

Hagafen Cellars
4160 Silverado Trail, Napa
707-252-0781 ⊙

Helena View/Johnston Vineyards
3500 Hwy 128, Calistoga
707-942-4956 ☎

Imagery Estate Winery
14335 Hwy 12, Glen Ellen
877-550-4278 ⊙
www.imagerywinery.com

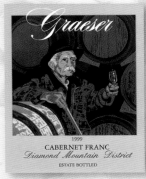

Graeser Winery
255 Petrified Forest Road,
Calistoga
707-942-4437 ⊙

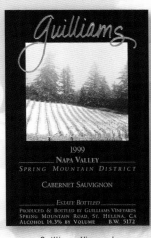

Guilliams Vineyards
3851 Spring Mountain Road, St. Helena
707-963-9059 ⊙

Harrison Vineyards
1527 Sage Canyon Road, St. Helena
707-963-8271 ✖

Hartford Family Wines
8075 Martinelli Road, Forestville
707-887-1756 ⊙
www.hartfordwines.com

Hendry Winery
3104 Redwood Road, Napa
707-226-2130 ☎

⊙ Open to the public, please call for hours.   ☎ Open to the public by appointment only, please call ahead.   ✖ Closed to the public.

64

Jarvis Winery
2970 Monticello Road, Napa
707-255-5280 ☎

Jordan Vineyard & Winery
1474 Alexander Valley Road, Healdsburg
707-431-5250 ☎
www.jordanwinery.com

Joseph Phelps Vineyards
200 Taplin Road, St. Helena
707-963-2745 ☎
www.jpvwines.com

KAZ Vineyard & Winery
233 Adobe Canyon Road, Kenwood
707-833-2536 ☎
www.kazwinery.com

Kelham Winery
360 Zinfandel Lane, St. Helena
707-963-2000 ☎

Kent Rasmussen Winery
1001 Silverado Trail, St. Helena
707-963-5667 ☎

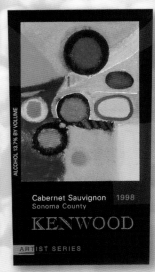

Kenwood Vineyards
9592 Sonoma Hwy, Kenwood
707-833-5891 ☉
www.kenwoodvineyards.com

Kirkland Ranch Winery
1 Kirkland Ranch Road, Napa
707-254-9100 ☉
www.kirklandwinery.com

F. Korbel and Brothers Champagne Cellars
13250 River Road, Guerneville
707-824-7316 ☉
www.korbel.com

Koves-Newlan Vineyards & Winery
5225 Solano Avenue, Napa
707-257-2399 ☉

Kunde Estate Winery & Vineyards
10155 Sonoma Hwy, Kenwood
707-833-5501 ☉
www.kunde.com

Ladera/Chateau Woltner
150 White Cottage Road, Angwin
707-965-2445 ☎

Lake Sonoma Winery
9990 Dry Creek Road, Geyserville
707-473-2999 ☎
www.lakesonomawinery.net

Lang & Reed Wine Company
PO Box 662, St. Helena
707-963-7547 ✖

Ledson Winery & Vineyards
7335 Sonoma Hwy, Santa Rosa
707-833-2330 ☎
www.ledson.com

Liparita Cellars
410 Lafata Street, St. Helena
707-963-2775 ✖

Livingston-Moffett Wines
1895 Cabernet Lane, St. Helena
800-788-0370 ☎

Luna Vineyards
2921 Silverado Trail, Napa
707-255-5862 ☉

Lynmar Winery
3909 Frei Road, Sebastopol
707-829-3374 ☎
www.lynmarwinery.com

Madonna Estate/Mont St. John
5400 Old Sonoma Road, Napa
707-255-8864 ☉

Markham Vineyards
2812 N. St. Helena Hwy, St. Helena
707-963-5292 ☉

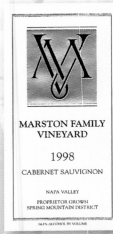

Marston Family Vineyards
3600 White Sulphur Springs Road,
St. Helena
415-472-3900 ☎

Matanzas Creek Winery
6097 Bennett Valley Road, Santa Rosa
707-528-6464 ☉
www.matanzascreek.com

☉ Open to the public, please call for hours.   ☎ Open to the public by appointment only, please call ahead.   ✖ Closed to the public.

Mayacamas Vineyards
1155 Lokoya Road, Napa
707-224-4030 ☉

Mazzocco Vineyards
1400 Lytton Springs Road, Healdsburg
707-433-9035 ☉
www.mazzocco.com

McCray Ridge
1960 Dry Creek Road, Healdsburg
707-869-3147 ☎

McKenzie-Mueller Vineyards & Winery
2530 Las Amigas Road, Napa
707-252-0186 ☎

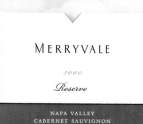

Merryvale Vineyards
1000 Main Street, St. Helena
707-963-7777 ☉
www.merryvale.com

Michel-Schlumberger
4155 Wine Creek Road, Healdsburg
707-433-7427 ☎
www.michelschlumberger.com

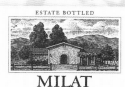

Milat Vineyards
1091 St. Helena Hwy, St. Helena
707-963-0758 ☉

Monticello Vineyards/Corley Family Napa Valley
4242 Big Ranch Road, Napa
707-253-2802 ☉
www.CorleyFamilyNapaValley.com

Moss Creek Winery
6015 Steel Canyon Road, Napa
707-252-1295 ☎

Mount Veeder Winery
Franciscan Oakville Estate
1999 Mt. Veeder Road, Napa
707-963-7111 ☉

Mumm Napa Valley
8445 Silverado Trail, Rutherford
707-967-7700 ☉

Murphy-Goode Estate Winery
4001 Hwy 128, Geyserville
707-431-7644 ☉
www.murphygoode.com

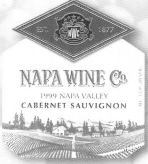

Napa Wine Company Sales Room
7830-40 St. Helena Hwy, Oakville
707-944-8669 ☉

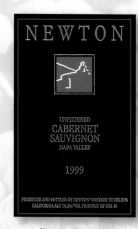

Newton Vineyard
2555 Madrona Avenue, Napa
707-963-9000 ☎

Opus One
7900 St. Helena Hwy, Oakville
707-944-9442 ☎

Pahlmeyer
PO Box 2410, Napa
707-255-2321 ✖

Pedroncelli Winery
1220 Canyon Road, Geyserville
707-857-3531 ☉
www.pedroncelli.com

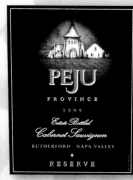

Peju Province
8466 St. Helena Hwy, Rutherford
707-963-3600 ☉
www.peju.com

Peterson Winery
1040 Lytton Springs Road, Healdsburg
707-431-7568 ☎
www.petersonwinery.com

Philip Togni Vineyard
3780 Spring Mountain Road, St. Helena
707-963-3731 ☎

Phoenix Vineyards & Winery
3175 Dry Creek Road, Napa
707-255-1971 ☎

Quintessa
1501 Silverado Trail, Napa
707-252-1280 ✖

Quivira Vineyards
4900 West Dry Creek Road, Healdsburg
707-431-8333 ☉
www.quivirawine.com

Rabbit Ridge Vineyards
3291 Westside Road, Healdsburg
707-431-7128 ☉
www.rabbitridgewinery.com

Pezzi King Vineyards
3805 Lambert Bridge Road, Healdsburg
707-431-9388 ☉
www.pezziking.com

☉ Open to the public, please call for hours.　☎ Open to the public by appointment only, please call ahead.　✖ Closed to the public.

66

Ravenswood Winery
18701 Gehricke Road, Sonoma
707-933-2332 ◉
www.ravenswood-wine.com

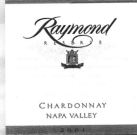

Raymond Vineyard & Cellar
849 Zinfandel Lane, St. Helena
800-525-2659 ☎
www.raymondwine.com

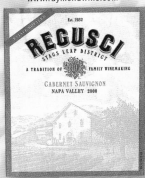

Regusci Winery
5584 Silverado Trail, Napa
707-254-0403 ◉

Reverie
1520 Diamond Mountain Road, Calistoga
707-942-6800 ☎

Reynolds Family Winery
3266 Silverado Trail, Napa
707-258-2558 ◉

Robert Craig Wine Cellars
830 School Road, #14, Napa
707-252-2250 ✖

Robert Keenan Winery
3660 Spring Mountain Road, St. Helena
707-963-9177 ◉

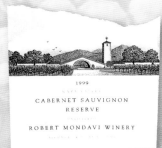

Robert Mondavi Winery
7801 St. Helena Hwy, Oakville
707-226-1395 ◉

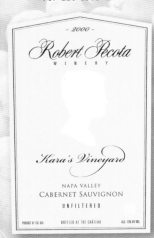

Robert Pecota Winery
3299 Bennett Lane, Calistoga
707-942-6625 ◉

Robert Sinskey Vineyards
6320 Silverado Trail, Yountville
707-944-9090 ◉

Robert Young Estate Winery
4960 Red Winery Road, Geyserville
707-431-4811 ☎
www.ryew.com

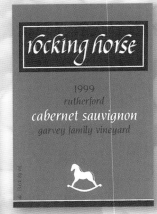

Rocking Horse Winery
PO Box 5868, Napa
707-226-5555 ☎

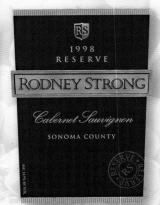

Rodney Strong Vineyards
11455 Old Redwood Hwy, Healdsburg
707-431-1533 ◉
www.rodneystrong.com

Rombauer Vineyards
3522 Silverado Trail, St. Helena
800-622-2206 ◉

Rosenblum Cellars
250 Center Street, Healdsburg
707-431-1169 ◉
www.rosenblumcellars.com

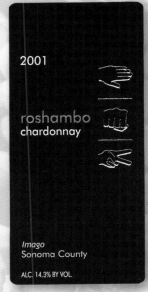

Roshambo Winery
3000 Westside Road, Healdsburg
888-525-WINE ◉
www.roshambowinery.com

Round Hill Vineyards
1680 Silverado Trail, St. Helena
707-963-9503 ◉

RustRidge Winery
2910 Lower Chiles Valley Road
St. Helena
707-965-9353 ◉

Rutherford Grove Winery
1673 St. Helena Hwy, Rutherford
707-963-0544 ◉
www.rutherfordgrove.com

Rutherford Hill Winery
200 Rutherford Hill Road, Rutherford
707-963-1871 ◉

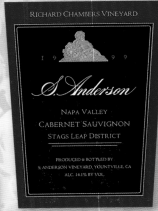

S. Anderson Vineyard
1473 Yountville Crossroad, Yountville
707-944-8642 ◉

Saintsbury
1500 Los Carneros Avenue, Napa
707-252-0592 ☎

Sawyer Cellars
8350 St. Helena Hwy, Rutherford
707-963-1980 ◉

◉ Open to the public, please call for hours. ☎ Open to the public by appointment only, please call ahead. ✖ Closed to the public.

Schramsberg Vineyards
1400 Schramsberg Road, Calistoga
707-942-6668 ☉

Schug Carneros Estate Winery
602 Bonneau Road, Sonoma
800-966-9365 ☉
www.schugwinery.com

Schweiger Vineyards
4015 Spring Mountain Road, St. Helena
707-963-4882 ☎

SEBASTIANI

Sebastiani Vineyards & Winery
389 4th Street East, Sonoma
800-888-5532 ☉
www.sebastiani.com

Sequoia Grove Vineyards
8338 St. Helena Hwy, Rutherford
707-944-2945 ☉

Sherwin Family Vineyards
4060 Spring Mountain Road, St. Helena
707-963-1154 ☎

Siduri Wines
980 Airway Court, Suite C, Santa Rosa
707-578-3882 ☎
www.siduri.com

Silver Rose Cellars
400 Silverado Trail, Calistoga
707-942-9581 ☉

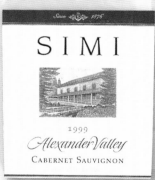

Simi Winery
16275 Healdsburg Avenue,
Healdsburg
707-433-6981 ☉

Sky Vineyards
1500 Lokoya Road, Napa
707-935-1391 ☎

Sonoma-Cutrer Vineyards
4401 Slusser Road, Windsor
707-528-1181 ☉
www.sonomacutrer.com

Spring Mountain Vineyard
2805 Spring Mountain Road, St. Helena
707-967-4188 ✖

St. Supéry Vineyard & Winery
8440 St. Helena Hwy, Rutherford
707-963-4507 ☉
www.stsupery.com

Stag's Leap Wine Cellars
5766 Silverado Trail, Napa
707-944-2020 ☉

Stags' Leap Winery
6150 Silverado Trail, Napa
707-944-1303 ✖

StoneStreet Winery & Tasting Room
337 Healdsburg Avenue, Healdsburg
707-433-7102 ☉

Stony Hill Vineyard
3331 N. St. Helena Hwy, St. Helena
707-963-2636 ☎

Storybrook Mountain Winery
3835 Hwy 128, Calistoga
707-942-5310 ☎

STERLING VINEYARDS

Sterling Vineyards
1111 Dunaweal Lane, Calistoga
707-942-3344 ☉
www.sterlingvineyards.com

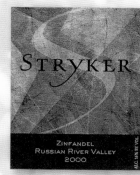

Stryker Sonoma Winery & Vineyards
5110 Hwy 128, Geyserville
707-433-1944 ☎
www.strykersonoma.com

Summers/Villa Andriana Winery
1171 Tubbs Lane, Calistoga
707-942-5508 ☉

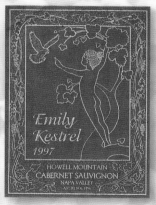

Summit Lake Vineyards & Winery
2000 Summit Lake Drive, Angwin
707-965-2488 ☎

Suncé Winery
1839 Olivet Road, Santa Rosa
707-526-9463 ☉
www.suncewinery.com

68

2000

NAPA VALLEY
MERLOT

Swanson Vineyards
1271 Manley Lane, Rutherford
707-967-3500 ☎

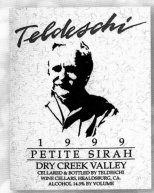

Teldeschi

1999
PETITE SIRAH
DRY CREEK VALLEY

F. Teldeschi Winery
3555 Dry Creek Road, Healdsburg
707-433-6626 ⊙
www.teldeschi.com

Trefethen

Trefethen Vineyards
1160 Oak Knoll Avenue, Napa
707-255-7700 ⊙

TRUCHARD
PINOT NOIR
CARNEROS
NAPA VALLEY

Truchard Vineyards
3234 Old Sonoma Road, Napa
707-253-7153 ☎

OLD VINE
Tudal
1998
Napa Valley
CABERNET SAUVIGNON
ESTATE BOTTLED

Tudal Winery
1015 Big Tree Road, St. Helena
707-963-3947 ☎

TULOCAY

2001
CARNEROS
CHARDONNAY

Tulocay Winery
1426 Coombsville Road, Napa
707-255-4064 ☎

UNTI
DRY CREEK VALLEY
SYRAH
2000

Unti Vineyards
4202 Dry Creek Road, Healdsburg
707-433-3104 ☎
www.untivineyards.coma

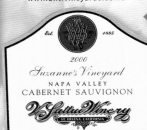

2000
Suzanne's Vineyard
NAPA VALLEY
CABERNET SAUVIGNON
V. Sattui Winery

V. Sattui Winery
1111 White Lane, St. Helena
707-963-7774 ⊙
www.vsattui.com

Valley of the Moon
Syrah

Valley of the Moon Winery
777 Madrone Road, Glen Ellen
707-996-6941 ⊙
www.valleyofthemoonwinery.com

1997
VAN DER HEYDEN
Vineyards
Napa Valley
Cabernet Sauvignon

Van Der Heyden Vineyards
4057 Silverado Trail, Napa
707-257-0130 ⊙
www.vanderheydenvineyards.com

VIADER
NAPA VALLEY SYRAH

Viader Vineyards & Winery
1120 Deer Park Road, Deer Park
707-963-3816 ☎

VINCENT ARROYO
WINERY

2000
JOY'S CHOICE
NAPA VALLEY
RED TABLE WINE

Vincent Arroyo Winery
2361 Greenwood Avenue, Calistoga
707-942-6995 ⊙

2000
VON
STRASSER
Cabernet Sauvignon
DIAMOND MOUNTAIN
DISTRICT
Napa Valley

Von Strasser Winery
1510 Diamond Mountain Road, Calistoga
707-942-0930 ⊙

WATTLE CREEK
SHIRAZ
ALEXANDER VALLEY
1998

Wattle Creek
25510 River Road, Cloverdale
707-894-5166 ☎

WELLINGTON
VINEYARDS
ESTATE BOTTLED
2001
SONOMA VALLEY
ZINFANDEL
100 YEAR OLD VINES

Wellington Vineyards
11600 Dunbar Road, Glen Ellen
707-939-0708 ⊙
www.wellingtonvineyards.com

2000
WHITE OAK
Merlot
ALEXANDER VALLEY
FOUNDED 1981

White Oak Vineyards
7505 Hwy 128, Healdsburg
707-433-8429 ⊙
www.whiteoakwines.com

WHITE ROCK
VINEYARDS
2000 NAPA VALLEY CHARDONNAY

White Rock Vineyards
1115 Loma Vista Drive, Napa
707-257-7922 ☎

WHITEHALL LANE
WINERY
2000
NAPA VALLEY
CABERNET SAUVIGNON

Whitehall Lane Winery
1563 St. Helena Hwy, St. Helena
707-963-9454 ⊙
www.whitehalllane.com

1999 RESERVE
WILLIAM HILL
WINERY
NAPA VALLEY
CABERNET SAUVIGNON

William Hill Winery
1761 Atlas Peak Road, Napa
707-224-4477 ⊙

YOAKIM BRIDGE
DRY CREEK VALLEY
ZINFANDEL
1998
Estate Bottled

Yoakim Bridge Vineyards & Winery
7209 Dry Creek Road, Healdsburg
707-433-8511 ☎
www.yoakimbridge.com

Zahtila Vineyards
Sonoma County
Zinfandel
Dry Creek Valley
Old Vines
2000

Zahtila Vineyards
2250 Lake County Hwy, Calistoga
707-942-9251 ⊙
www.zahtilavineyards.com

ZD WINES
2000
ZD
Pinot Noir
CARNEROS

ZD Wines
8383 Silverado Trail, Napa
800-487-7757 ⊙
www.zdwines.com

NAPA VALLEY

Arger-Martucci Vineyards
1455 Inglewood Avenue, St. Helena
707-963-4334 ☉

Azalea Springs Vineyards
4301 Azalea Springs Way, Calistoga
707-942-4811 ✖

Bell Wine Cellars
6200 Washington Street, Yountville
707-944-1673 ☉

Blockheadia Winery
1764 Scott Street, St. Helena
707-963-8593 ☎

Buehler Vineyards
820 Greenfield Road, St. Helena
707-963-2155 ☉

Burgess Cellars
1108 Deer Park Road, St. Helena
707-963-4766 ☎

Cafaro Cellars
1591 Dean York Lane, St. Helena
707-963-7181 ☎

Cardinale Estate
1600 St. Helena Hwy, Oakville
707-944-2807 ☉

Carneros Creek Winery
1285 Dealy Lane, Napa
707-253-9463 ☉

Charles Krug Winery
2800 Main Street, St. Helena
707-967-2200 ☉

Chateau Chevre
2030 Hoffman Lane, Yountville
707-944-2184 ☎

David Arthur Vineyards
1521 Sage Canyon Road, St. Helena
707-963-5190 ☎

Deer Park Winery
1000 Deer Park Road, Deer Park
707-963-5411 ☉

Del Dotto Caves
1055 Atlas Peak Road, Napa
707-256-3332 ☎

Domaine Chandon
1 California Drive, Yountville
707-944-8844 ☉

Dominus Estate
2570 Napanook Road, Yountville
707-944-8954 ✖

Ehlers Grove/Cartlidge & Brown Winery
3220 Ehlers Lane, St. Helena
707-963-3200 ☉

Elyse Wineries
2100 Hoffman Lane, Napa
707-944-2900 ☉

Far Niente
1350 Acacia Drive, Oakville
707-944-2861 ✖

Frank Family Vineyards
1091 Larkmead Lane, Calistoga
707-942-0859 ☉

Frog's Leap
8815 Conn Creek Road, Rutherford
707-963-4704 ☉

Grace Family Vineyards
1210 Rockland Road, St. Helena
707-963-0808 ☎

Groth Vineyards & Winery
750 Oakville Crossroad, Oakville
707-944-0290 ☉

Hakusan Sake Gardens
1 Executive Way, Napa
707-258-6160 ☉

Hans Fahden Vineyards
5300 Mountain Home Ranch Road, Calistoga
707-942-6760 ☉

Harlan Estate
1551 Oakville Grade, Oakville
707-944-1441 ☎

Hess Collection Winery
4411 Redwood Road, Napa
707-255-1144 ☉

Jessup Cellars
3377 Solano Avenue, Suite 402, Napa
707-224-7067 ☎

Joel Gott
1458 Lincoln Avenue, Railcar #15, Calistoga
707-942-1109 ☎

Jones Family Vineyard
PO Box 352, Calistoga
707-942-0467 ☎

Judd's Hill
PO Box 415, St. Helena
707-963-9093 ☎

Juslyn Vineyards
2900 Spring Mountain Road, St. Helena
707-967-8020 ☎

Kuleto Villa Winery
2470 Sage Canyon Road, St. Helena
707-963-9750 ✖

La Famiglia di Robert Mondavi
1595 Oakville Grade, Oakville
707-944-2811 ☉

Laird Family Estate
5055 Solano Avenue, Napa
707-257-0360 ☉

Larkmead Vineyards
1145 Larkmead Lane, Calistoga
707-942-6605 ☎

Leducq Vineyards & Winery
3222 Ehlers Lane, St. Helena
707-963-5972 ☉
www.leducq.com

Long Meadow Ranch Winery
1775 Whitehall Lane, St. Helena
707-963-4555 ✖

Long Vineyards
PO Box 50
707-963-2496 ☉

Louis M. Martini Winery
254 St. Helena Hwy, St. Helena
707-963-2736 ☉

Mario Perelli-Minetti/W. Harrison Vineyards
1443 Silverado Trail, St. Helena
707-963-8310 ☉

Miner Family Vineyards
7850 Silverado Trail, Oakville
707-944-9500 ☉

Napa Cellars
7481 St. Helena Hwy, Oakville
707-944-2565 ☉

Nichelini Winery & Tasting Room
2950 Sage Canyon Road, St. Helena
707-963-0717 ☉

Niebaum-Coppola Estate Winery
1991 St. Helena Hwy, Rutherford
707-968-1100 ☉

Noah Vineyards
6204 Washington Street, Yountville
707-944-0675 ☎
www.noahvineyards.com

Oakford Vineyards
1575 Oakville Grade, Oakville
707-945-0445 ☎

Paoletti Estates Winery
4801 Silverado Trail, Calistoga
707-942-0689 ☎

Paradigm Winery
683 Dwyer Road, Oakville
707-944-1683 ☎

Pine Ridge Winery
5901 Silverado Trail, Napa
707-253-7500 ☉

Plumpjack Winery
620 Oakville Crossroad, Oakville
707-945-1220 ☉

Pope Valley Winery
6613 Pope Valley Road, Pope Valley
707-965-1246 ☎
www.popevalleywinery.com

Prager Winery & Port Works
1281 Lewelling Lane, St. Helena
707-963-7678 ☉

Ristow Estate
5040 Silverado Trail, Napa
415-931-5405 ☎

Ritchie Creek Vineyard
4024 Spring Mountain Road, St. Helena
707-963-4661 ☎

St. Clement Vineyards
2867 N. St. Helena Hwy, St. Helena
707-967-3033 ☉

Saddleback Cellars
7802 Money Road, Oakville
707-944-1305 ☎

Screaming Eagle
PO Box 134, Oakville
707-944-0749 ✖

Seavey Vineyard
1310 Conn Valley Road, St. Helena
707-963-8339 ☎

Shafer Vineyards
6154 Silverado Trail, Napa
707-944-2877 ☉

Showket Vineyards
7778 Silverado Trail, Oakville
707-944-9553 ✖

Signorello Vineyards
4500 Silverado Trail, Napa
707-255-5990 ☉

Silverado Hill Cellars
3105 Silverado Trail, Napa
707-253-6160 ☉

Silverado Vineyards
6121 Silverado Trail, Napa
707-259-6641 ☉
www.silveradovineyards.com

Smith-Madrone Vineyards & Winery
4022 Spring Mountain Road, St. Helena
707-963-2283 ☉

Spottswoode Winery
1902 Madrona Avenue, St. Helena
707-963-0134 ☎

Staglin Family Vineyard
1570 Bella Oaks Lane, Rutherford
707-944-0477 ☎

Star Hill Winery
1075 Shadybrook Lane, Napa
707-255-1957 ☎

Steltzner Vineyards
5998 Silverado Trail, Napa
707-252-7272 ☎

Stonegate Winery
1183 Dunaweal Lane, Calistoga
707-942-6500 ☉
www.stonegatewinery.com

Stonehedge Winery
1242 East Avenue, Napa
323-780-5929 ✖

Sullivan Vineyards
1090 Galleron Lane, Rutherford
707-963-9646 ☉

Sutter Home Winery/Trinchero Family Estates
277 St. Helena Hwy, St. Helena
707-963-3104 ☉

Turnbull Wine Cellars
8210 St. Helena Hwy, Oakville
707-963-5839 ☉

Van Asperen Vineyards
1680 Silverado Trail, St. Helena
707-963-5251 ☉

Vigil Vineyards & Winery
3340 Hwy 128, Calistoga
707-942-2900 ☉

Villa Helena Winery
1455 Inglewood Avenue, St. Helena
707-963-4334 ☉

Vine Cliff Winery
7400 Silverado Trail, Napa
707-944-2388 ☉

Vineyard 29
2929 Hwy 29 North, St. Helena
707-963-9292 ✖

Vintner's Collective (representing several
  small producers)
1245 Main Street, Napa
707-255-7150 ☉
www.vintnerscollective.com

Wermuth Winery
3942 Silverado Trail, Calistoga
707-942-5924 ☉

Whitford Cellars
4047 East 3rd Avenue, Napa
707-942-0840 ☎

☉ Open to the public, please call for hours.   ☎ Open to the public by appointment only, please call ahead.   ✖ Closed to the public.

SONOMA

A. Rafanelli Winery
4685 West Dry Creek Road, Healdsburg
707-433-1385 ☎

Alexander Valley Vineyards
8644 Hwy 128, Healdsburg
800-888-7209 ☎
www.avvwine.com

Amphora Winery
5540 West Dry Creek Road, Healdsburg
707-431-7767 ☎
www.amphorawines.com

Artisan Cellars (serving wines from several
  small producers)
337 Healdsburg Avenue, Healdsburg
707-433-7102 ☉

Bartholomew Park Winery
1000 Vineyard Lane, Sonoma
707-935-9511 ☉
www.bartholomewparkwinery.com

B.R. Cohn Winery
15140 Sonoma Hwy, Glen Ellen
707-938-4064 ☉
www.brcohn.com

Canyon Road Winery
19550 Geyserville Avenue, Geyserville
707-857-3417 ☉
www.canyonroadwinery.com

Carmenet Vineyard
14301 Arnold Drive, Glen Ellen
707-996-5870 ☎

Cellar Door Tasting Room at the Lodge at
  Sonoma
1395 Broadway, Sonoma
707-938-4466 ☉

Chateau St. Jean
8555 Sonoma Hwy, Kenwood
707-833-4134 ☉
www.chateaustjean.com

Chateau Souverain
400 Souverain Road, Geyserville
888-809-4637 ☉
www.chateausouverain.com

Christopher Creek Winery
641 Limerick Lane, Healdsburg
707-433-2001 ☉
www.christophercreek.com

Deerfield Ranch Winery
1310 Warm Springs Road, Glen Ellen
707-833-5215 ☉
www.deerfieldranch.com

Deux Amis Winery
1960 Dry Creek Road, Healdsburg
707-431-7945 ☎
www.deuxamiswines.com

Domaine Saint George
1141 Grant Avenue, Healdsburg
707-433-5508 ☎
www.domainesaintgeorge.com

Family Wineries of Sonoma Valley
9200 Hwy 12, Kenwood
707-833-5504 ☉
www.familywineries.com

Field Stone Winery
10075 Hwy 128, Healdsburg
707-433-7266 ☉
www.fieldstonewinery.com

Foppiano Vineyards
12707 Old Redwood Hwy, Healdsburg
707-433-7272 ☉
www.foppiano.com

Forchini Winery
5141 Dry Creek Road, Healdsburg
707-431-8886 ☎

Forth Vineyards
2335 West Dry Creek Road, Healdsburg
707-473-0553 ☎

Gan Eden Wines
4950 Ross Road, Sebastopol
707-829-5686 ☎
www.ganeden.com

Hafner Vineyard
PO Box 1038, Healdsburg
707-433-4606 ☎

Hanna Winery
9280 Hwy 128, Healdsburg
707-431-4310 ☎
www.hannawinery.com

Hanzell Vineyards
18596 Lomita Avenue, Sonoma
707-996-3860v
www.hanzell.com

Hart's Desire Wines
25094 Asti Road, Cloverdale
707-579-1687 ☎

Iron Horse Vineyards
9786 Ross Station Road, Sebastopol
707-887-1507 ☉
www.ironhorsevineyards.com

J Wine Company
11447 Old Redwood Hwy, Healdsburg
707-431-3646 ☉
www.jwine.com

J. Rochioli Vineyards and Winery
6192 Westside Road, Healdsburg
707-433-2305 ☉

Johnson's Alexander Valley Wines
8333 Hwy 128, Healdsburg
707-433-2319 ☉
www.johnsonwines.com

Joseph Swan Vineyards
2916 Laguna Road, Forestville
707-573-3747 ☉
www.swanwinery.com

Kendall-Jackson Wine Center
5007 Fulton Road, Santa Rosa
707-571-8100 ☉
www.kj.com

Lambert Bridge Winery
4085 West Dry Creek Road, Healdsburg
707-431-9600 ☉
www.lambertbridge.com

Lancaster Estate Winery
15001 Chalk Hill Road, Healdsburg
707-433-8178 ☎
www.Lancaster-reserve.com

Landmark Vineyards
101 Adobe Canyon Road, Kenwood
707-833-0053 ☉

Limerick Lane Cellars
1023 Limerick Lane, Healdsburg
707-433-9211 ☉

Martinelli Winery
3360 River Road, Windsor
707-525-0570 ☉

Martini & Prati Wines
2191 Laguna Road, Santa Rosa
707-823-2404 ☎
www.martiniprati.com

Meeker Vineyards
21035 Geyserville Avenue, Geyserville
707-431-2148 ☉
www.meekervineyards.com

Mill Creek Vineyards
1401 Westside Road, Healdsburg
707-431-2121 ☉

Moon Mountain Vineyard
1700 Moon Mountain Drive, Sonoma
707-996-5870 ☎
www.moonmountainvineyard.com

Paradise Ridge Winery
4545 Thomas Lake Harris Drive, Santa Rosa
707-528-9463 ☉
www.paradiseridgewinery.com

Pastori Winery
23189 Geyserville Avenue, Cloverdale
707-857-3418 ☉

Porter Creek Vineyards
8735 Westside Road, Healdsburg
707-433-6321 ☉

Pride Mountain Vineyards
9155 St. Helena Road, Santa Rosa
707-963-4949 ☎

Preston Vineyards
9282 West Dry Creek Road, Healdsburg
707-433-3372 ☉
www.prestonvineyards.com

Raymond Burr Vineyards
8339 West Dry Creek Road, Healdsburg
888-900-0024 ☉

Ridge Vineyards
650 Lytton Springs Road, Healdsburg
707-433-7721 ☉
www.ridgewine.com

Roche Winery
28700 Arnold Drive, Sonoma
707-935-7115 ☉

Sable Ridge Vineyards
6326 Jamison Road, Santa Rosa
707-528-1921 ☎

Sapphire Hill
51 Front Street, Healdsburg
707-431-1888 ☉
www.sapphirehill.com

Sausal Winery
7370 Hwy 128, Healdsburg
707-433-2285 ☉
www.sausalwinery.com

Sebastopol Vineyards/Dutton Estate
8757 Green Valley Road, Sebastopol
707-829-9463 ☉
www.sebastopolvineyards.com

Seghesio Family Vineyards
14730 Grove Street, Healdsburg
707-433-3579 ☉
www.seghesio.com

Selby Wines
5 Fitch Street, Healdsburg
707-431-1703 ☉
www.selbywinery.com

Silver Oak Cellars
24625 Chianti Road, Geyserville
707-857-3550 ☉
www.silveroak.com

Sonoma Creek
23355 Millerick Road, Sonoma
707-938-3031 ☎

Stone Creek Wines
9380 Sonoma Hwy, Kenwood
707-833-5070 ☉
www.stonecreekwines.com

Stuhmuller Vineyards
4951 West Soda Rock Lane, Healdsburg
707-431-7745 ☉

St. Francis Winery & Vineyards
100 Pythian Road, Santa Rosa
800-543-7713 ☉
www.stfranciswine.com

Taft Street Winery
2030 Barlow Lane, Sebastopol
707-823-2049 ☉

Talty Winery
7127 Dry Creek Road, Healdsburg
707-433-8438 ☉
www.taltyvineyards.com

Topolos at Russian River Vineyards
5700 Gravenstein Hwy, Forestville
707-887-1575 ☉
www.topolos.com

Trentadue Winery
19170 Geyserville Avenue, Geyserville
707-433-3104 ☉
www.trentadue.com

Verité Winery
4611 Thomas Road, Healdsburg
707-433-9000 ☎
www.veritewines.com

Viansa Winery & Italian Marketplace
25200 Arnold Drive/Hwy 121, Sonoma
707-935-4700 ☉
www.viansa.com

Wilson Winery
1960 Dry Creek Road, Healdsburg
707-433-4355 ☎

Windsor Vineyards
308B Center Street, Healdsburg
707-433-2822 ☉
www.windsorvineyards.com

The Wine Room
9575 Hwy 12, Kenwood
707-833-6131 ☉
www.the-wine-room.com

CHAMBERS OF COMMERCE

Healdsburg Chamber of Commerce &
  Visitors Bureau
217 Healdsburg Avenue, Healdsburg
707-433-6935 or 800-648-9922

Mendocino Coast Chamber of Commerce
332 N. Main Street, Fort Bragg
707-961-6300 www.mendocinocoast.com

Napa Valley Conference & Visitors Bureau
1310 Napa Town Center, Napa
707-226-7459 www.napavalley.com

Napa-Sonoma Wine Country Visitor
  Services Center
707-642-0686 or 800-877-5904

Russian River Chamber of Commerce &
  Visitors Bureau
16209 First Street, Guerneville
707-869-9000 www.russianriver.com

Sonoma County Tourism Program
520 Mendocino Avenue, Suite 210
Santa Rosa
800-5-SONOMA or 707-565-5383
www.sonomacounty.com

Sonoma Valley Visitors Bureau
453 First Street East
and 25200 Arnold Drive, Sonoma
707-996-1090 www.sonomavalley.com

The Wine Center
5000 Roberts Lake Road, Rohnert Park
707-586-3795 www.sonomawine.com

Yountville Chamber of Commerce
707-944-0904 www.yountville.com